WOMEN OF BENGAL

WOMEN OF BENGAL

MARGARET M. URQUHART

WITH ILLUSTRATIONS

GYAN PUBLISHING HOUSE
New Delhi - 110002

WOMEN OF BENGAL
ISBN : 9788121200080

Published in 2014 in India by
Gyan Publishing House
23, Ansari Road, Daryaganj,
New Delhi - 110002
Phones : 23261060, 23282060 Fax : 23285914
e-mail : books@gyanbooks.com
website : gyanbooks.com

Laser Typesetting at : Vinayak Printers, Delhi
Printed at : Salasar Imaging System, Delhi

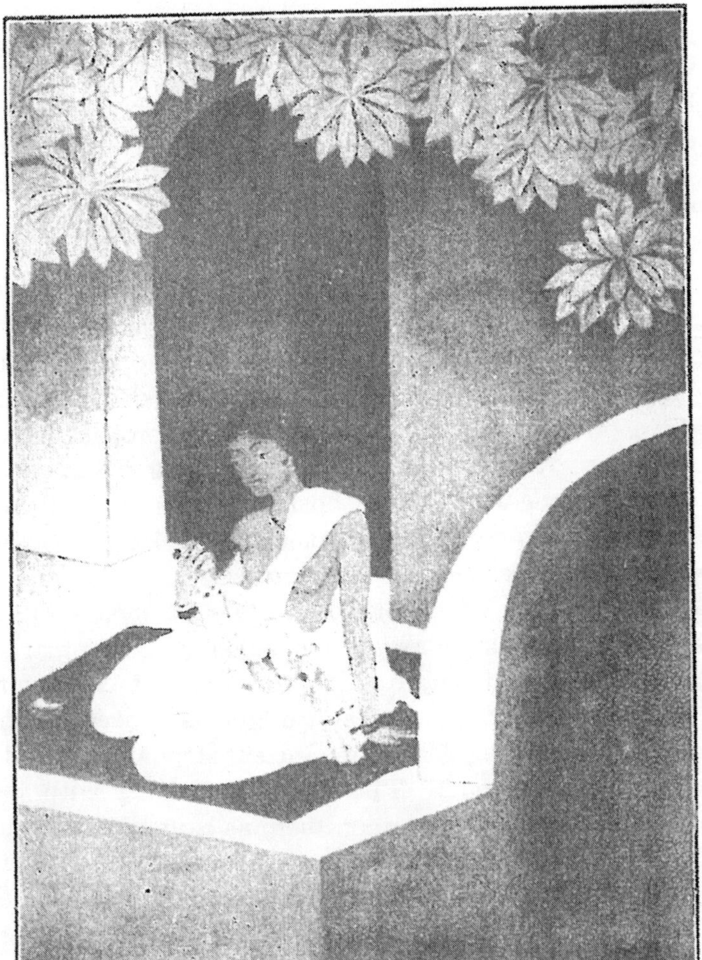

THE NEW BORN.

From the picture by Satyendra Nath Banerjee.

PREFACE TO THE FIRST EDITION

SOME years ago Professor J. N. Farquhar, now of Manchester University, invited me to write a book about Bengali women, which was to form one volume of a projected series on the women of India. A number of promises had been given, but, so far, no other volume has appeared, and it is with some hesitation that I allow mine to be the first to be published, since there is no series in existence to explain its appearance. I can only express a hope that it will be followed by other descriptive books of a similar nature.

My endeavour has been, in the small compass of this sketch, to give a picture of the Bengali woman in her natural setting, the Bengali home. Considerable misunderstanding has arisen in the past through placing her side by side with women of other, especially Western, races, and judging her character and the conditions of her life by means of contrast only. If she loses rather than gains by the comparison, this has been due, in my opinion, to the unfair character of the test. A very different result might have been obtained by measuring her against more ancient standards: Biblical, classical, or mediæval. The West is familiar with these standards and still looks upon them as examples to follow. Indian ideals of womanhood bear a much closer relation to ancient than to modern types, and, although the achievement of a race usually falls far short of its ideals, it is still true that a people may be judged by its heroes and heroines, for by studying these we see the embodiment of its highest conception of character. Indian heroines are second to those of no other race in nobility and grace of character, and they are continually set before the young women of Bengal as objects for veneration and imitation. "Make me a wife like Sītā," is a prayer taught to girls, and Sītā, goddess though she be, makes her appeal, like Sāvitrī and others, by the human qualities of wifely devotion and purity.

The vernacular literature of Bengal is not without its heroines of romantic love, but, in the main, it is woman as wife, humble, selfless and faithful, who is enshrined in the hearts of the people. The most beautiful building in India, perhaps in the world, the Taj Mahal, celebrates an emperor's devotion to a beloved wife, and this may be taken as a clue if we would find where the romance of Indian lives often lies hidden.

A "wise passiveness" is a distinguishing trait in the character of Bengali women. Passivity has its victories as well as activity, and perhaps in India more than in any other country do we find the faith that to be passive, to be non-resistant, is to wield the greatest of all forces. This faith is the true *satyāgraha.* It explains the appeal of Mr. Gandhi's teaching to millions of hearts. To "endure all things" is, to the mind of the typical woman of India, the mark of great love.

This sketch is limited to the women who have come within the range of my own experience during a residence of twenty-five years in Bengal—the caste women of Calcutta and its surroundings. The connection of most Calcutta Hindu families with rural Bengal is, however, still so close, that my descriptions, in so far as they are true, will to a large extent apply equally to village women. With many of these *pardānaśins*[1] whom I have known I think I may claim

[1] Secluded women.

that my relation has been not merely that of a spectator or a teacher, but one of friendship and real intimacy. Without this first-hand acquaintance, it would be presumption to attempt a description of Bengali home-life and character; with it, one may at least essay the task, although conscious of gaps in one's knowledge and of inevitable misinterpretation. The motive of writing at all is a genuine desire to gain and to pass on a better understanding of the life of our fellow-subjects in Bengal than is within reach of most Europeans in India.

No one can become familiar with the women of Bengal without learning much from the simplicity and piety of their lives. The virtues of the olden time still shine in the ways of many a well-ordered Hindu household, and the Hindus have good cause to be proud of their womenfolk. I should like to offer this book as a tribute to the sweetness and strength that I have found within the walls of Calcutta's homes, and as an expression of gratitude for the happiness that has come to me from the intercourse I have been allowed to enjoy with the dwellers in these homes.

My cordial thanks are due to Professor J. N. Farquhar, at whose instigation and with whose generous encouragement I have ventured to begin and finish this book; to Pandit Kalipada Mukherjee, who taught me the Bengali language and whose mind is richly stored with Indian lore of which I have made but poor use in this limited sketch; without his willing help I should scarcely have attempted the task of describing the Bengali woman and her life; to Miss Marie Gasper, of the Church of Scotland Women's Mission, for reading the manuscript and giving useful criticism; to the present proprietors of the *Calcutta Review*, for permitting me to use the substance of articles written by me under a pen-name and published in their pages under its former management, and also for permission to reproduce the photograph of the late Srimati Kamala Devi; to Mr. Rama Prasad Mookerjee, the brother of the latter, for obtaining the consent of his family to the use of this picture as illustration of a Brāhman lady; to Srimati Jyotirmoyee Devi, for permission to publish her photograph; to Miss B. Hardie, for the photograph of a Hindu pilgrim; and to others who have lent photographs for which acknowledgment is made below the reproductions; to Mr. Satyendra Nath Banerjee, for permission to use his picture as frontispiece; and to Mr. H. Mazumdar, for the cover design and his picture facing page 96; to Mr. O. C. Gangoly, Editor of *Rupam*, for permission to reproduce from that magazine two pictures by Mr. J. Seal; to my husband for revision and advice; and to many Indian friends who have answered questions from time to time.

Scottish Churches College,
Calcutta,
October, 1925.

M.M.U.

PREFACE TO THE SECOND EDITION

It is a pleasure to learn that a second edition of this book is called for. I am grateful to the public and to the Press, both Indian and European (in India), for the kind reception they have given to my attempt to draw a picture of Bengali home life. The British reviews which have reached me are cordial, and the sale of the book in Britain seems to indicate that there exists a demand for information of this kind, and that interest in all that refers to India is becoming more widespread.

The way in which Hindus and other Bengalis in conversation, or by letters, have privately shown their appreciation of the motive which prompted me to write, has been a source of happiness to me. In some of the reviews certain critical remarks of mine have been misunderstood or resented. One review complained that I did not criticise English women. But English women are not the subject of the book. In the main, however, I have been given credit, especially by Hindu writers, for accuracy in the statement of my facts and for a sympathy which it was my purpose to express, and which I hope I may claim to possess.

Except for minor alterations, the book remains unchanged.

Calcutta,
March, 1926.

M.M.U.

CONTENTS

CHAPTER I

THE BACKGROUND

THE character of races is, to some extent at least, the result of their physical environment. This is a mere truism, but it is one often forgotten in our judgment of people of other lands. Travellers cannot fail to observe that, even in the same person, vigour waxes or wanes, moods constantly change, and the mind itself is affected, under varying climatic conditions. Who has not felt an immediate rise in his spirits as he emerged from the cold fogs of the English Channel into the sunshine and warmth of more southerly seas, and watched in his fellow-passengers a similar transformation from dullness to gaiety? These transient moods of the traveller indicate, it may be, the general temperament of the races inhabiting the zones through which he is passing. We leave behind, in the northern parts of the British Isles, the gravity and moroseness of the Scottish Highlander, who finds little to laugh at in a grey world; and discover, in the south of Europe, the nonchalance and playfulness of the Spaniard and Neapolitan, who see very little to be serious about in a world full of sunlight.

In a land like Bengal we find a curious blend of these qualities. It may be more accurate to say, not that they blend, but that they exist side by side. Dazzling sunshine is seldom absent except in the monsoon season, but the sunshine although cheering, is too fierce, and the heat too intense, for comfort. Consequently, we note in the people extremes of light-heartedness and despondency, puzzling to the foreigner until he begins to feel in himself the same unaccountable variations of mood. The brilliant light is robbed of its joy-giving effect by the bodily fatigue and mental lassitude resulting from excessive heat and humidity combined. The healthy-minded foreigner, unwilling to admit defeat, meets the attack by energetic measures such as violent physical exercise and sport; but the people of the land succumb passively both to physical inertia and a pensive, if not gloomy, frame of mind, which tends to become habitual.

Climate and country are not, of course, the only factors in forming racial character. Prevailing ideas, especially of a religious nature, wield a powerful influence in the creation of distinguishing traits. These ideas may come from without, breaking into a race's history with dynamic force, as was the case, for example, with Islam in India or Buddhism in Japan, and, although of alien origin, may have effects as marked as those which make the Muhammadans of India differ so fundamentally from their Hindu compatriots as to appear almost like another race. But, more usually, prevailing ideas come from within and are gradually evolved and stereotyped from the thought-life of the race itself; when they are so derived, it is often difficult to distinguish between cause and effect, and to say whether the religious belief has produced the racial character or the racial character the religious belief.

The racial origins of the peoples of Bengal are obscure. The noticeably fair strain is supposed to be predominantly Mongolian. The Bengali Brāhmans, however, claim to be Aryan, and regard the Śūdras as of a different race. On these points Mr. O'Malley writes: "There are three main stocks, namely Dravidian, Mongolian and Aryan. . . . The oldest races are the Dravidians, who survive, like an island in a sea of alien races, in the hilly country of Chota Nagpur, the Orissa States and the Santal Parganas. The Mongolians are found in the mountainous country to the extreme north and south-east of Bengal, and there is also a strong Mongoloid strain in some of the tribal castes of the plains of Bengal. Lastly, there is the Aryan element, which has modified the original type in nearly all parts, the higher castes having the strongest and the lower castes the weakest infusion of Aryan blood. . . . Altogether, four types are distinguished by ethnologists on the basis of anthropometrical data, namely Aryo-Dravidian, Mongolo-Dravidian, Mongoloid and Dravidian."[1]

Through careful marriage in certain castes and classes, the fair strain, accompanied by beauty of feature, is outstanding. Partly from a desire to shield this beauty from the darkening effects of sunburn, and partly from an inability to bear the direct rays of the sun, women of the wealthier classes are content to be "hidden from the sun," and no doubt seclusion may have begun accidentally, as it were, in this perfectly natural way. The usual explanation given is the fact that the women of the Moghul conquerors were secluded, and Indian women had likewise to be protected.

The trend of social, religious and political life in Bengal reveals a race highly-strung, quickly elated and easily depressed, rising suddenly into a frenzy of public emotion and excited activity, and lapsing again just as suddenly into a mood of indifference or even despair. To the Bengali in the first state the comparative stolidity of the British

[1] *Bengal, Behar and Orissa, Sikkim*, L. S. S. O'Malley, pp. 174-5.

temperament, with its hatred of expressed emotion, is a source of intense irritation. But in the mood of reaction the volatile Indian turns with relief to the equanimity of the Englishman, no longer taunting him with lack of imagination and feeling, but prizing his imperturbability as something to " bank on " in an unstable world.

We hear frequently of a recent golden age—all golden ages are, of course, pre-British—when the Bengalis were a healthy, stalwart, and contented race. But there is nothing to prove this legend, and a good deal to cast doubt upon it. The more warlike races of India have for a very long time looked upon the Bengali as not greatly to be reckoned with either as a foe or an ally. Mr. O'Malley quotes an up-country proverb which says: "Go to Europe for manufactures, and to Bengal for talk." In justice to the Bengalis, however, it must be said that during the War it was the ambition of their youths to disprove the truth of such strictures by demanding the formation of a Bengali regiment, and by volunteering in many capacities for the Front. Bengal has produced a refined and intellectual, but not an aggressive race. It is doubtful if the Gangetic plain will ever be a favourable breeding ground for peoples with the staying power of those born in more invigorating regions. Yet it is noteworthy that in the intellectual professions, and in peaceful avocations of a clerical kind, the Bengali has invaded the north-west.

Bengalis are sometimes accused of being indolent. This is a question not to be decided off-hand by outsiders. The systole and diastole of activity and rest are different in different individuals and peoples, and there is really no norm which can be applied as an absolute test. The pulse, figuratively speaking, is shorter in the people of the north, and longer in those of hot countries. The Indian peasant will work with persistence and patience at a wearisome task, hour after hour, going without food for periods that would entirely exhaust an Englishman ; but these long periods are balanced by corresponding seasons of complete idleness.[1] For the agricultural labourer in India such terms of idleness are often enforced by drought or flood, when no field work is possible. The enforced leisure becomes a habit not easily unlearned when the peasant engages in some other kind of employment. In a country so rich in grain products the struggle for existence is not severe, and an easy temper is natural. Another possible cause of the periods of slackness is that the staple food of Bengal is not sufficiently nourishing or stimulating, and after a spell of hard toil, reserves are exhausted and have to be renewed by complete rest. Similar habits are noticeable in the women, who spend hours on end doing absolutely nothing. This may be nature's way of making up the losses entailed in early and frequent child-bearing, and the fatiguing processes of cooking and housework in the great heat.

When not at work, Indians, men or women, will sleep anywhere, at any time; no bed is too hard. Even if not asleep, they indulge in a suspension of activity and thought that almost amounts to coma.

The British "Tommy" is credited with describing his sensations when stationed in Calcutta as "being under the Bengal blanket." The figure is sufficiently apt for those who have shared his experiences. But this is merely the impression of aliens whose constitution, diet, and habits of dress are not designed for a land like India. The English-

[1] A certain "fecklessness" characterises the Indian masses in their method of work. They are unwilling to spend money on new implements or better ones, or to improve their system. This results in unproductiveness and general poverty. Cf. *India in 1924-25*, L. F. Rushbrook Williams, p. 238.

man's stiff garments and his conservative attachment to a diet devised for cold countries do not help matters. For the son of the soil, however, the climate has its subtle charms, and he sees in the powerful beams of the sun and the moisture-laden winds the beneficent forces of nature which draw forth miracles of teeming life, and create the "splendours of Bengal" of which the poet Tagore sings. The sentiment of devotion to Bengal is expressed in the words of a song much sung in recent days: "She is the queen of all lands—the land of my birth."

The Hindu year is divided into four main seasons corresponding to those of the temperate zone, but these are thought of in six periods. The spring is short and full of the beauty of vivid foliage and flowering forest trees. Growth is sudden and rapid, and fresh thunder-showers wash away the signs of the monotonous and dusty cold season. As in other lands, the spring inspires the poet and the artist, and the common folk have their gay and sometimes Saturnalian revels in the festival of *Holi* and the *Saṁkrānti* pantomimes. For the women the later spring has its pleasures in the sweet-smelling flowers that may be gathered for worship, and in the ripening of certain fruits to a degree sufficient for making the acid preserves which last throughout the year and serve as an appetising and cooling accompaniment to their somewhat oily diet. *Vaiśākh*, beginning in mid-April, is a specially sacred month for women, and it is believed that conjugal union at such a time will be blessed with fruitfulness.

One of the women's rites connected with this season is the giving of fruits and prepared sweets to Brāhmans; another is the making of offerings of food to a married woman who has her feet dyed with red lac and her hair anointed and dressed. The cow is specially tended also at this time, and bamboo shoots and other delicate food given to her.

In the spring the heat is great during, the day, but the nights are cooled by the south wind which blows inland from the distant sea. It is a time of sweet scents from the blossom-laden trees, and of clear starlit and moonlit nights. After one of the great storms known as Nor'westers, alarming to newcomers on account of their terrific thunder and incessant lightning, but welcome to all for the coolness they bring, the nights are sometimes of such beauty as to satisfy one's utmost dreams. The happiness caused by these conditions finds expression among the Bengalis in special gatherings on the night of the full moon of *Basanta* for music and song, and in recent days the reading by bards of their poems.

After the period of storms comes the real hot season, too fierce for the gentle name of summer. In the scorching rays of the sun the ground becomes baked and white. The thick foliage hangs limply on the trees, and the myriads of crows gasp with wide-open beaks, too thirsty to keep up the raucous chorus which is one of the minor trials of life in Indian cities. The daily temperatures rise above 100 degrees in the shade, sometimes reaching 108 degrees or more during heat waves, and in the heart of the city as much as 115 degrees. Inside the mud-walled cottages and small houses of the people there is no coolness anywhere. The whole population, Indian and European, resigns itself to durance vile. Those who can do so, escape to the hills. The rest count the days till June brings the monsoon, with its mighty rain-burst and cloudy skies.

It is worth noting in this connection that the almost insupportable temperatures of midsummer have affected the metaphors of cold and hot as applied to persons. A cold or cool person is one who is gentle and soothing; a warm temperament is an excitable and restless one.

With the coming of the rains all nature revives, and the people breathe again. The dust-filled air is washed clear. The pavements and walls, which radiated heat long after sunset, are bathed and cooled in the deluge of rain. The trees grow green once more and vegetation springs up with amazing luxuriance. Since the food supply and much of the wealth of Bengal depend on a good monsoon, the season is welcomed and celebrated in songs and poems. After a time, however, the great humidity, accompanied by higher temperatures than at the first break of the rains, begins to tell upon the population, already wearied by the hot season. Everyone suffers from growing lassitude, loss of appetite, and the minor irritations of "prickly heat," boils, and other symptoms of an overheated system. For those who are not robust the season is peculiarly trying, but it has its compensations in the absence of dust and glare, and the refreshing greenness of grass and foliage. To the housewife the season is welcome because the warfare with dust ceases for a time, although a fresh campaign opens against mould and hordes of destructive insects. All woollen materials and other fabrics must be laid away in air-tight boxes, with herbs or chemicals to ward off these insect foes. Everything else in use, such as bedding, must be frequently sunned or dried on a frame over a brazier. Possessions of the kind that Europeans set store by, such as carpets and hangings, books, shoes and leather articles, etc., quickly deteriorate, and one realizes the wisdom of the Oriental, who keeps his house as bare as possible. Towards the end of September the moisture-laden winds cease to blow. The sun's heat grows excessive once more, and causes an evaporation from the sodden

Photograph by Edna Lorenz.

A "RAINS" SKY OVER CALCUTTA.

The Victoria Memorial in the Maidan of Calcutta is visited daily by Bengali ladies, who arrive mostly in closed garis or in motors. The photograph shows three Hindu girls, who do not observe strict parda, seated among the marble pillars.

earth that makes the atmosphere extremely oppressive. Only the prospect of the cool season, now in sight, makes this period bearable.

Some of the greater Hindu festivals fall in a group in October and November, and it is the chief holiday season for Indians. Those who are absent from their village homes return there. It is the occasion for family reunions and general rejoicings. In its spirit of goodwill and family festivity the season resembles our Christmastide. Presents are given and received, especially of new, bright clothing for the young folk. The cessation of the rain makes possible open-air celebrations in courtyards, or on the roof, and the sight of fields of grain ripening in the autumn sun[1] and other signs of plenty, cheer the heart of the householder, so that in the minds of all Hindus a peculiar happiness is associated with this *pūjā*[2] season. The cool season which follows is greatly prized by the European, but not so much by Bengalis, and especially their womenfolk. Their dwellings and clothing are not adapted to cold winds, nor are their constitutions quickly tempered to the chill fogs of December and January. For the women, in most cases, no additional garments are provided, and, although the naturally robust develop a certain hardiness, the majority, owing to the kind of life they are obliged to live, suffer from chills and all their accompanying evils, especially dysentery, cholera and kindred ailments.

[1] When the milky substance first appears in the swelling ears of rice the cultivators make an offering of *sādh* (good things to eat), such as is given to expectant mothers in the ninth month of pregnancy, while they sing, "Mother Lakshmi (Indian Ceres) has entered the womb of the rice."

[2] Religious feast.

With their thin cotton *sāṛīs*, bare feet and wet hair (they souse their heads in the daily bath) the Bengali women look very pitiable on a cold day. Their usual seat is the mud or cement floor, often without even the luxury of a mat, except in the houses of the well-to-do. At night the thin quilt, filled with cotton down, which takes the place of a blanket, is not a sufficiently warm protection against the penetrating mists. Consequently, to keep warm, the people close their windows and doors—a practice even more dangerous to health in India than in colder countries because there are no chimneys to ventilate the rooms, and epidemics of a highly infectious kind are prevalent. The mosquitoes, which have their best opportunity for biting at night, accumulate in swarms where there is no through current of air. The *hīm*, or cold dew of winter, is regarded as the agent of most of the diseases peculiar to the season, and one must protect one's self against it at all costs. "Mad, quite mad," was the comment of an old Bengali, who saw a bed in my house placed in an open verandah. "Who is so foolhardy as to expose life to danger in this way?" Bengalis do not realize that, while such trivial ailments as a cold in the head or a crick in the neck may be avoided by shutting windows, in the close atmosphere of the room where, sometimes, a whole family of parents and little children sleep together, germs of far deadlier ills are being bred, and every life exposed to the danger of tuberculosis, which is becoming a scourge in Calcutta.

Spasmodic efforts, mostly of a private character, are made from time to time to acquaint ignorant people with these dangers to domestic health and the way to avoid them. But people will be warm, in spite of leaflets on hygiene, and warnings fall on deaf ears. If the Bengali poor possessed more coverings from the cold, they would be more ready to listen. At the same time, there is a curious indifference to discomfort and an unwillingness to make the necessary efforts to remove it.[1] Someone has divided the human race into "putters-up, and non-putters-up," and one is inclined to class the Bengalis among the former. An intelligent young Hindu expressed to me recently a regret that Bengalis were wearing more clothing than formerly, and wished that they could return to the simple life and "one-cloth" standard of comfort. Cheap woven underwear, manufactured in Japan and now also in Indian factories, is a boon—whatever may be thought of its æsthetic value—and is much in vogue for schoolboys and students.

One aspect of the environment of the Bengali woman's life which must always be remembered is its physical dangers. Coming from climes where nature is more benign, the foreigner in India is struck at once by the terrors that lurk everywhere. Wherever the forest encroaches, or deep rivers pass the villager's door, tigers, leopards, wolves and crocodiles are an occasional menace and cause deaths every year. Great numbers of peasants are killed by snakes.[2] Sunstroke and death from lightning are common occurrences; and scarcity and contamination of water cause famine and cholera, from which some part or other of the

[1] "The real truth is that the undeniable poverty of India arises principally from the fact that the country is governed by a tradition which does not recognise the production and accumulation of wealth as being among man's legitimate aims. Accordingly, the prevalent social system does not encourage either the habit of mind or the method of life upon which the successful pursuit of material prosperity in the last resort depends." *India in 1924-25*, L. F. Rushbrook Williams.

[2] Over 22,000 persons were killed by wild animals (including venomous snakes) in British India, in 1924.

country is never free. Floods are another ever-dreaded catastrophe in certain districts. In a night not only one's dwelling but even one's fields may be swept away; and in hilly regions the bare foundation of rock on which soil has been laid with infinite toil is all that is left to the heart-broken cultivator. Along with these natural calamities there are the visitations of fell diseases, plague, smallpox, malaria, kala-azar and other fatal ills, which claim their victims by thousands, sometimes within a small area. It is little wonder that the minds of the masses are possessed by fear, kept in control only by a pathetic fatalism that has to serve for courage.

Such, in bare outline, is the physical background against which we must view the life of the women of Bengal, a background rich and varied and in many ways alluring, but one which, for the reasons indicated, makes a great demand upon endurance, both physical and mental. The very richness of their land constitutes a danger. "The fertility of a country may prove its ruin, if accompanied by a soft and languid climate which saps the energies and weakens the combative instincts of the inhabitants."[1]

Like the country which she loves, and whose sacred soil and holy streams she worships, the Bengali woman reveals in her character sharp contrasts of light and shade, benignity and passion, an attempt to delineate which will be made in the following chapters.

[1] *Peoples and Problems of India*, T. W. Holderness, p. 8.

From a drawing by L. M. Ghose.

A BENGAL RIVER SCENE.

. . . My boat,
On the calm Padma's peaceful breast afloat,
Sways in the liquid plash ; in distance gleam
Half sunken sands, like creatures of the stream
Sprawling at bask ; high, crumbled bluffs ; and trees
Dark with deep shade, and hidden cottages.
A narrow, winding path its streak has worn
From some far hamlet through the fields of corn,
And dips to the water like a tongue athirst.
The village women, to the throat immersed,
Shrill gossip hold, their garments drifted round ;
Their high, sweet laughter makes one rippling sound
. . . with the light waves . . .

—RABINDRANATH TAGORE,
Translated by Edward Thompson

CHAPTER II

THE HOME

HOUSES in Bengal are of two types, known as *kāncha*, literally raw or unripe, and *pākā*, that is, cooked or ripe, the words corresponding roughly to the idea of temporary and permanent buildings. The first are composed of mud and bamboo, the second of brick and cement. The words have also come to be used in many connections, to denote what is sound or unsound in work or character.

The great mass of the people of Bengal live in kāncha or "earth houses" as they call them, a name which we have translated as mud huts. Properly constructed and kept in good repair, these cottages are neat and comfortable, and compare very favourably for convenience with the homes of European peasantry. It is not considered undignified for people of good caste and birth to live in such houses, although families of social standing usually have more substantial headquarters.

The cost of building a mud house is, or at least was, very small, the material being at hand in field and forest, and the art of building common knowledge among the villagers. A homestead of this kind, large enough to accommodate a family of, let us say, four brothers, their wives and families, could, half a century ago, be built for about fifty rupees. The same house would now cost a sum nearer three hundred rupees—about twenty pounds. Bamboos and a few stout beams, mother earth and the stubble of the rice fields, are all the materials required. A lattice of bamboo strips forms the windows, which are protected from sun and rain by the broad eaves. The floors are of beaten mud.

The rooms of the house are grouped round and open on an enclosed courtyard, giving an inward and not an outward view. This very fitly symbolizes, and perhaps even helps to explain, the self-contained and exclusive character of Bengali family life.[1] Bengalis as a rule show themselves lacking in what may be called community sense, social bonds being with caste-fellows rather than neighbours. The central space ensures light and air. The rooms are placed, and the doors and windows constructed, so as to catch the prevailing winds. On the sunward side a mud platform, shaded by a projecting roof on bamboo supports, makes an open-air sitting-room, and protects the walls from the direct rays of the sun during the hottest period of the day.

The following description of the detailed arrangements of a typical village home is taken from the pages of *Bengal Peasant Life*:[2] "On the west side of the yard . . . stands the *bara ghar*, or big hut. This is the biggest, the neatest, and most elaborately furnished. . . . Its walls, which are of mud, are of great thickness. The thatch, which is of the straw of paddy,[3] is more than a cubit deep; . . . the middle beam which supports the thatch, though it is neither of the costly teak or *śāl*,[4] is made of the pith of the palmyra; and the floor is raised at least five feet from the ground. The hut is about sixteen cubits long and twelve cubits broad, including the verandah. . . . The verandah is the parlour of the family. There friends and acquaintances sit on mats. In Badan's[5] sleeping room

[1] *Vide infra*, p. 30. [2] By Lal Behari Dey. [3] Rice.
[4] An Indian tree. [5] The hero of the story.

are kept the brass vessels of the house and other valuables. There is no *khāṭ* or bedstead in it, for Badan sleeps on the mud floor, a mat and a quilt stuffed with cotton interposing between his body and mother earth. . . . I need scarcely add that there is no furniture in the room—no table, no chairs, no stools, no almirahs,[1] no wardrobe, no benches; there is only in one corner a solitary wooden box. On one side of the room two whole bamboos are stuck in the walls, on which clothes are hung and on which the bedding is put up in the day."

The other portion of the house is composed of the cook-room and the "*āntuṛ ghar*," or lying-in room. This latter is sometimes constructed as need arises, by screening off a portion of the courtyard with leaf matting. The cowhouse is occasionally used, a practice that helps to explain the manger at Bethlehem. After the mother and child have finished the days of separation, the matting and the contents of the room are destroyed. A similar room is sometimes made to hold the *dhenki*, or pedal for husking rice, a lever with a peg at one end on the lower side which pounds the grains placed in a hole. It is worked by the foot, and is a slow but effective method of husking. The girls of the household usually have charge of this primitive instrument. Alongside of the living room is the cowhouse, also opening on to the courtyard. In the centre of the yard stands the small Indian granary or *gola*, built of bamboo strips and thatch to hold the household supply of grain from harvest to harvest.

Brick houses, such as one sees in the small towns and in Calcutta, and here and there among the villages on the larger land-holdings, are built on the same general plan,

[1] Cupboards.

the chief difference being that, with the stronger structure, it is possible to have houses of two or three storeys. This means cooler rooms on the ground floor, the well-like court acting as a funnel and ventilating the lower rooms. When a house is placed at the proper angle to avoid sun and catch the breezes, these ground floor rooms can be kept surprisingly cool for the greater part of the year.

But even large cities like Calcutta are by no means entirely composed of brick buildings. Long ago Calcutta was described as "the city of mud huts and palaces," and the description is still an apt one. Large towns in India often begin by being a fortuitous concourse of villages or *pārās*, and different parts of the city are to this day so described, the separate sections being known as the pārā of the tailors or cobblers, or other trades which have settled there, or simply by the name of a clan whose headquarters increase till they form a little village. As these words are being written the writer looks down from a building of four storeys on a tract of land covered with "earth" houses of the most rustic sort. Every year sees the removal of some of these, as new sites are required for buildings of a more urban type.

The mud hut has something to be said for it as a hygienic dwelling, because it is at least thoroughly penetrated by air and sunlight—and this is not the case with some of the tall tenements now built in great numbers in Calcutta.

The typical dwelling-house of the *bhadra-lok*, or better class people, has two courts (one behind the other) instead of the one open yard of the rural homestead. The front court is the larger, and on it open the more important rooms, which usually form a building of one storey. These courts are paved with brick, cement or marble, according to the means of the occupant. The outer court takes the place of the hall of an English house, being a kind of open-air reception room, where domestic and religious festivals are held. On special occasions the space is roofed in by heavy cloths to make a pavilion, so that the company may be sheltered from sun and rain. This improvised roof is lined with printed fabric and other embellishments and makes a handsome setting for suspended lights and festoons of yellow marigolds, which on gala nights are sometimes used for decoration. In the houses of the wealthier classes the outer court is spacious, and the architectural effect of its arcaded loggias and galleries is imposing. At one end the verandah forms a deep recess, where, during the Hindu religious feasts, the newly made image of clay and straw is set up, decorated and worshipped.

Round the outer court are the public rooms, the chief of which is the *baithak khānā*,[1] often a spacious and marble-floored apartment, where the men of the house receive their friends, and where the hookah, symbol of social intercourse, is smoked. A man knows that he is ostracised when the hookah is not passed to him. The *daftar* or office, the boys' schoolroom, and the library, if there is one, make up the men's portion of the house. The keeping of private libraries is not, as far as I have been able to observe, a habit among Hindus. As in ancient times in Europe, books and manuscripts are the possessions of religious schools and monasteries. But, with the introduction of Western learning and habits of scholarship, the custom of having one's own library is on the increase. The development of Bengali literature also makes it a mark of cultivation to possess the works of well-known modern vernacular writers or Bengali writers in English.

[1] Sitting-room.

The outer court is usually, except in the poorer sort of house, large enough to catch the sunshine, so that the rooms surrounding it are bright and pleasant owing to the reflected light. It has a half-social, half-sacred character for the inmates, since the portion dedicated to the household worship is holy ground and in strictly orthodox families must be trodden barefoot. In the great houses of the aristocracy the "family chapel" is a separate temple, on which great treasure is sometimes lavished. The daily worship in a household is usually carried on in a small chamber on the roof, where the image or symbol is kept.

The inner court is the women's quarter, and very often the contrast between it and the front portion recalls a facetious description of a modern English villa as having a "Queen Anne front and a Mary Ann back." It is unadorned, usually shabby, and often mean-looking and cramped. Light and air are deficient, and the lower rooms, where the women carry on most of their domestic tasks, cooking, baking, and cleaning utensils, are often stuffy and insanitary. Calcutta houses often have one storey in front and two behind, so that the sleeping quarters may be above the ground level. Upstairs there is more brightness; and, if the flat roof is accessible, women and children have one means of getting fresh air and sunning themselves and their belongings. But where seclusion is strict, the roof, if overlooked by other houses, is considered too public for the use of the women.

To many of the pardānaśins of Calcutta, cooped up day in day out, "cribbed, cabin'd and confined" in the stifling heat of the city, life is mere existence, such as we, with our notions of freedom and variety, would hardly think good enough for a horse or a dog. But it is necessary to remember that this is not the view taken of it by the women themselves. Sister Nivedita, in one of her sketches of Calcutta life, thus describes the inner court: "Standing without in the noonday hush, and looking into the semi-darkness of the women's apartments, it is as if one caught a glimpse of some convent garden full of rare and beautiful flowers . . . true it is that silence and shadow are the ideals of the life of Eastern womanhood." Miss Noble saw all things Indian through rose-coloured glasses; and, although all who know it admit the flower-like qualities of the best Bengali womanhood, it is doing the women no service to idealise the almost intolerable conditions in which many of them are condemned to pass their days. Better is the realism of the zealous officer of public health, who writes in a very different vein: "In spite of the improvement in the general death-rate of the city, the death-rate amongst females is still more than forty per cent. higher than amongst males. . . . This inversion of the usual ratio between male and female death-rates is a remarkable feature of the vital statistics of the city. Until it is realized that the strict observance of the *pardā* system in a large city, except in the case of the very wealthy, who can afford spacious homes standing in their own grounds, necessarily involves the premature death of a large number of women, this standing reproach to the city will never be removed. . . . The whole excess mortality among females occurs amongst young women in the prime of life. . . . The heavy mortality from respiratory diseases and tuberculosis amongst women is clear proof of the deadly effect of depriving them of fresh air and light by confining them in the zenana, which . . . is always the most insanitary part of the house. The women's apartments are always the inner apartments, and being constructed with the sole object of securing privacy, adequate lighting and ventilation are secondary considerations."[1]

Alike in rural and town houses, one is struck by the absence of furniture. But this must be taken as a mark of simplicity rather than penury. In hot countries, where houses cannot be closed to keep out dust and rain, and where coolness and space are the first essentials of comfort, bareness is desirable and hygienic. Western influences have changed the standards of the moneyed classes, who imitate European styles; but in the great majority of homes, and even among old-fashioned wealthy people, a room is considered amply furnished with a thin mattress laid on the floor and covered with a clean white sheet. Over the mattress are scattered hard sausage-shaped cushions, on which to recline. This is a style usually reserved for the men's rooms. The women's apartments are even more Spartan, and have no sort of seat at all except a grass mat, which is unrolled for visitors. The women themselves sit, as a rule, on the bare floor.

This ability to do without things is a matter of pride to Indians, and some of their greatest men deliberately adopt a style of stark simplicity. The writer has been received by ladies of high caste and ancient lineage, whose habits of sitting, dressing and eating have an attractive austerity. When, owing to damp, it is not convenient to sit on the floor, a raised platform of wood, the *taktaposh*,[2] is used

[1] *Calcutta Health Officer's Report, 1917*. In his report for 1923 the same officer writes: "Between the ages of 15 and 20 years, for every boy that dies of tuberculosis, five girls die. What is the reason for this truly appalling state of affairs? Well, to put it brutally, these girls were suffocated behind the pardā . . . another very important factor, as regards tuberculosis amongst girls and young women, is early marriage."

[2] The *pirhī*, a low stool, is also used for guests and at meal times. It is a seat of honour, although so lowly.

both for sitting and sleeping. During the day the quilts and mats, which are required at night, are rolled up and put aside. It is an easy matter for a Bengali woman to "take up her bed and walk."

The Bengali housewife, habituated for generations to a traditional custom and routine, has not yet adapted herself to the introduction of Western styles of furnishing. Heavy bedsteads and cupboards, tables and chairs, upholsteries and hangings, form a problem with which she has not been trained to cope. The menfolk, when they make money, are tempted by such things in European shops and desire to add to the glory of their state by introducing foreign luxuries into their houses. The result is that, in many cases, the simple housewife finds her home encumbered with unwieldy articles, for the care of which neither she nor her domestics have any rule, and which stand almost unused, gathering dust and fingermarks, and becoming infested with bugs until they are an eyesore to behold and a source of discomfort, and it may be of disease—if the bug is guilty of the ills some theories ascribe to it.

The old-fashioned taktaposh and mats could be thoroughly sunned and aired, but heavier articles are apt to become fixtures, and make hiding place for mosquitoes. The emancipated women, who move about among houses conducted on more modern lines, and who have been educated for a different style of living, have a more adequate idea of keeping things in order ; but in many houses dust, cobwebs, and a general air of neglect and disrepair rob these superfluous furnishings of any charm. The average Bengali house offers a complete contrast to our ideas of Oriental luxury, and it is difficult to understand whence these ideas are derived.

Observation of illiterate and literate housewives forces upon one the conclusion that some degree of education almost invariably improves a woman's standards of order and her housewifely capacity. Many of the uneducated women of Calcutta exhibit a childish indifference to method, cleanliness and punctuality. In the East, time is generally a very lightly prized commodity. Ignorance of any standard but that of their own household, robs the women of the impulse to improve their surroundings, and they remain easily satisfied with things as they are. Segregation of households is apt to produce a dead level of dullness and discomfort. The elegance and cleanliness of the middle-class Western home is often the result of a healthy rivalry and a determination to be as good as, or better than, one's neighbour whose house one visits and admires. This stimulus is lacking where there is little social intercourse. Occasionally, however, one meets a housewife whose house is her pride. In such a case it is exquisitely kept.

Apart from the scant furnishings, a Bengali's chief household possessions are the cooking pots of iron, brass and earthenware, and the platters, drinking cups and goblets of bell-metal, in which food and beverages are served. In a place apart are the beautiful vessels for worship, made of silver, copper and brass. The plates and bowls used for food make the chief decoration of the house—although their purpose is not primarily decorative. They brighten and beautify the simplest dwelling, and it is matter for regret that in so many homes they are being replaced by hideous articles of enamel and other cheap ware. It would be a great loss to the artistic side of home life if the craft of making shapely and beautiful vessels of common use were no longer in demand.

These brass utensils form the wealth of rustic homes, and great is the outcry when one is stolen—as often happens. They are scoured after use with a wisp of straw dipped in water and ashes. Stains are removed by the acid pulp of tamarind pods, and the burnishing is done with the palm of the hand. This produces a soft brilliance more like gold than brass. In wealthy houses silver and even gold plates are used, but this is rare. The new bride is sometimes fed off a silver plate, and areca nut and spices are offered to distinguished guests in a silver bowl. An ornate sprinkler of silver is used for the ceremonial anointing of guests with attar of roses.

Foodstuffs, such as rice, oil and pulses, are kept in large earthenware jars. The cooking utensils are very few and simple, and the fireplace is of the most primitive kind, constructed of clay and of a beehive shape.[1] Beside this low *chula* the woman has to bend or squat, while round her on the floor are the kitchen articles. These consist, besides pots and pans, of a flat stone and grindstone, with which she pounds and mixes the spices, a pair of tongs for lifting the pots by the neck, a fishslice, a spoon for stirring the lentil broth, and a nutcracker to split the betel nut, which is chewed after meals every day.

It is a comparatively simple thing for an Indian family to move with all its possessions. For the poorest our picnic methods are a habit of frequent occurrence. One sees whole families "camping" in the shelter of railway stations. The modern station takes the place, for travellers, of the old *sarāi*, or resthouse, which used to mark the pilgrim routes and at which the wayfarer asked only space

[1] The people of India are extraordinarily conservative in the matter of implements and methods. Little attempt is made to save labour or to combine speed with efficiency. Cf. Footnote, p. 5.

enough to kindle a fire and stretch himself to sleep upon the ground.

Indian houses are usually devoid of hangings. Even the pardā, or veil, which one pictured as drawn in front of the women's quarters, is as a rule figurative rather than actual. On festive occasions split bamboo screens are hung up, through which the women can see without being seen. In theatres and other public places, where women may be present, thick mosquito netting is used for the same purpose.

When a pardā woman has to speak to a man outside of her family, a curtain is hung up and she stands behind it, and when visited by a male doctor a woman patient is covered up with a sheet, and the doctor has to make his diagnosis as best he can without seeing her. If it is necessary for a woman to step outside her house to enter a carriage or *palanquin*, a private passage is made by holding up two sheets. In important houses, where the ladies drive out daily in a closed carriage, such cloths are kept in readiness by the *darwān*, or gate porter. For ordinary folk, in the same circumstances, it is sufficient for the lady to muffle up her face and figure in a sheet or shawl. At the present day one sometimes sees in Calcutta motor cars with their hoods up and with cotton sheets draping the opening and knotted securely. As these sheets billow out in the wind the cars have the appearance of boats in full sail. Sometimes the knots get loosened and the sheets fly up, while the distressed ladies inside duck down with their shawls over their heads, lest they should be visible for one moment to the passers-by.

The embroideries and covers made in Kashmir, and other fine Indian work so much admired in Europe, are very little used by Bengalis. They seem to be made mostly for foreigners. In other parts of India *phūlkaris*, which

Photos by B.K.H. and C.M.H. TOWN AND COUNTRY LIFE. *Photo by Houghton-Butcher.*

(1) Main court of a large Calcutta house, with women's palanquin ready for an outing; below, interior court where the women live.

(2) On the right is a Bengal village scene, with a sacred pipal tree growing beside the tank.

English people use as curtains, are actually the common dress of the woman; but not in Bengal. The Kashmir shawl with its finely worked border, and the famous sāṛīs of Benares and Madras are almost the only products of other provinces in general use. The shawl is worn by men more than by women.

As far as I have observed, the only stitchery known to the women, unless they have learned to do European "fancy" work, is the making of bed quilts and mats from worn-out sāṛīs. The sāṛīs are put together several ply thick, and bound by a network of stitches in various designs of flowers, animals and birds. The coloured threads in the border of the sāṛī are used for embroidery. This is a thrifty and artistic use to make of old clothes, and an industrious woman can produce elaborate and beautiful designs. Unfortunately, the younger women look upon this as grannies' work, and prefer crocheting and other foreign needlecraft. The Bengali girl loves stitchery, and when instructed works deftly at lace-making and other delicate work. Her taste is still very crude, however, and she has not learned to apply the art of decorative embroidery to the beautifying of her house or personal attire.

Home, in the fullest sense, always means for a Bengali one's own house and not a hired dwelling. To the question, "Where is your home?" one is often surprised to get the answer from some person brought up and even born in Calcutta—"In Jessore," or "In Dacca," or some other rural district. By this is meant that the family has its headquarters there, and owns land or at least a house in which parents or other senior relatives still reside.

Attachment to the birthplace of one's forebears is a very powerful sentiment among Bengalis, and explains to some extent the lack of what one might call civic consciousness.

Sojourn in a city is regarded by the majority of Indians as a mere temporary arrangement; for their hearts are still rooted in the village of their upbringing and the soil of their native district. The hereditary priests of the family are there, and the sacred symbols and images of worship, without which they cannot keep the great feasts of the Hindu year. If the husband is in the city and the wife in the country home, they cannot keep the family rites apart; for the wife is *sahadharminī*—"companion in religious observances." Hindu religious life consists in an outward-going pilgrimage to some celebrated sacred place and a return to the lares and penates and the family altar.

The patriarchal roof is thus beloved, not only for reasons of family and kinship, but because it is a place of intimate worship and hallowed religious association. In the mind of the Hindu, as he dreams of his family roof-tree, there will mingle the homely sounds of children's voices, the cooing of black pigeons—omens of prosperity if they make his house their gathering place—and the pungent smells of spiced cookery, with the solemn striking of the gong that calls the god to awaken, the scent of incense, and the chanting of the priest, as he repeats the sonorous *mantras* by which the god is invoked, or addresses the dead ancestors of the household on the occasion of obsequies or other solemn family events.

"Home" is often something very old, encrusted with memories of many generations, shabby and even decaying it may be, but making a peculiar appeal, blended of human and religious emotions, to the heart of the devout Hindu. Such sentiments can never attach to the rented town-house in the minds of those who have retained some connection with their hereditary district. But in this, as in all things, changes are very evident. There are now a great many families in Calcutta who have, for various reasons, severed that old bond, and in doing so have lost much that was admirable and vital to the preservation of some of the finest elements in Hindu family life. They have cut themselves off from the old religion of the hearth, and have in many cases failed to find a discipline or worship to take its place. There is a pathos to the observer in the spectacle of lives from which the dignity and happiness of the old order have passed away.

CHAPTER III

THE FAMILY

DEVOTION to family and obedience to caste rules must be reckoned as the principal controlling ideas in Bengali life. Duty to society in general comes a long way after these two loyalties, and a real sense of social responsibility is still rare in the orthodox Hindu. As one might expect, such a sense has scarcely dawned on the consciousness of the great mass of the women. Not long ago a Bengali pardānaśin, fond of airing her views on many topics, put the matter simply and vividly to the writer. "We Bengalis," she said, "are a selfish race. We have nothing to do with our neighbours. If the son of the house next door murders his mother, it is no concern of mine. I shut my ears and close my eyes to it. What are they to me?" She made these remarks in self-criticism, thus revealing a certain awareness that such an attitude is anti-social. The exaggeration was used, as it is so often by Indian women, simply for dramatic effect.

Yet one must set against this apparent indifference to the weal of the community the direct charities[1] which are enjoined on and practised by all orthodox families. "Throughout the year a stream of charity flows unceas-

[1] Both charity and hospitality occasionally have ulterior motives. This may be true everywhere, but specially so in the East, when the one is practised to acquire religious "merit," and the other very often to curry favour with possible benefactors.

ingly from all households in proportion to their several means. The unostentatious benevolence of all grades of society is one of the most beautiful traits of Indian life."[1]

The recipients of this bounty are the crowds of beggars, halt, maimed and blind, who haunt the Hindu shrines and temples, and every house and public place where family or religious festivals are being celebrated. Charity has created a beggar community of astonishing dimensions. It is said that they number at least five millions. Mr. Archer, in his book,[2] makes the curious reckoning that the upkeep of this multitude of parasites, at the rate of three rupees a head, may be computed at fifteen million rupees a month—about a million pounds sterling. This expenditure, as he points out, is entirely unproductive from an economic point of view, and only serves to produce more beggars. No doubt Hindus would take this argument as an example of the crass materialism of the West, for to their minds the beggar community does produce something all-important, the value of which cannot be counted in money. Do not the beggars provide by their very existence an easy means of acquiring religious merit, and is not religious merit the only wealth worth accumulating in this world? Sometimes, however, the gifts to beggars are worthless and the food given to poor dependents scant and wretched.

This consideration also justifies the beggar's existence to himself; for he believes that in receiving alms he confers a precious boon on the giver, and covers a multitude of his benefactor's sins in this and previous births. The true ascetic, who also receives alms, must be distinguished from ordinary beggars, for he is not willing to accept them from

[1] *Peoples and Problems of India*, T. W. Holderness, p. 142.

[2] *India and the Future*, William Archer.

all and sundry. "The poorest and most illiterate Brāhmans will not usually accept the gifts of a washerman, fisherman, vintner or courtesan."[1]

With all this undoubted benevolence—a benevolence curiously perfunctory and impersonal in its character—the Hindu family remains exclusive and self-contained, not readily admitting outsiders to its intimacies. In apparent contradiction to this statement is the courteous greeting of guests and the lavish hospitality which is *de rigueur* at all ceremonial entertainments connected with marriages, *Śrāddhas*,[2] and so forth. As an example of reticence may be taken the fact that it is not polite for one Indian gentleman to say to another, "How is your wife?" A general inquiry only is permitted, which may be translated: "What is the news of your home?" or "How are all your relatives?" The reply will also be in general terms, and where wife and daughters are concerned individual mention of them will not as a rule be made. In the same way a wife speaks of her husband indirectly as "the boy's father" or "the master of the house." If she uses the possessive my, it will be along with the dignified *swāmī*, literally lord, the usual title given to the husband. In these inhibitions there are doubtless traces of ancient taboos.

The English family, although deriving its name from the Roman *familia*, does not closely resemble the Latin institution; but in the Indian household of the present day we find an almost exact parallel to the ancient significance of the word. The social unit in India is not the individual but the family, and the family indicates not merely one human pair and their offspring, but the patriarchal group in

[1] *Hindu Castes and Sects*, J. N. Bhattacharya, p. 226.

[2] Death ceremonies.

its main stem and branches, including not only its living representatives but its dead ancestry also. One of the most important parts of a wedding ceremony, for instance, is that carried on with great care in both households concerned by the family priest, the symbolic feasting and propitiation of several generations of ancestors. The individual member is of value only in so far as he holds sacred and advances the interests of this group.

Under the old regime, which still holds sway for the great majority of Hindus, the joint-family system sometimes resulted in the existence of very large households. Even at the present day in Calcutta there are some old-fashioned establishments in which the number of souls runs into hundreds. The occupants of such houses are usually a family of brothers with their wives, their sons and daughters-in-law, their grandsons, who may also be married, with their wives and infants, and a great staff of servants to attend to the wants of all these persons. A feature of all such households, too, is the *pishimā*, the paternal aunt. In each generation represented, the girls or women who have become widows, although rightly belonging to the family of their dead husbands, prefer to live with their brothers, if their brothers' means permit, and if their sisters-in-law do not make it unpleasant for them.

An erroneous impression seems to persist among those unfamiliar with Hindu home-life that such households are a kind of harem, where the several wives of one husband live together. Polygamy is not forbidden to Hindus,[1] but in Bengal it is uncommon, and in Calcutta very unusual. The *Kulīn* Brāhmans used to marry many wives, and occasionally one comes across a woman who is one of two or even several wives. But, except in rare instances, these

[1] Cf. p. 40.

co-wives do not live together, but remain in their paternal home, where they are visited occasionally by their husbands.[1] Very often the husband, in such circumstances, feels no responsibility for supporting the wife. He has saved her from losing caste by marrying her, so her family is in a sense his debtor, and he expects them to acknowledge the debt by treating him with great respect, and feeding him on the fat of the land at such times as he chooses to acknowledge the relationship. Such a noble career as the rescue of maidens from social ostracism was considered not unworthy of the knights-errant of Kulīnism, and in former days many of them earned an "honourable" living in this way. But the Brāhman has fallen on evil days, and the profession of pluralist husband is no longer what it once was.

Where large households, such as have been described, exist, the control of so great a host of persons, young and old, requires a particular kind of authority, and a genius for exercising that authority; and for the several members of the household a very clearly defined relation to those at the head is necessary. Without such a discipline it would not be possible to secure order, peace, mutual respect and prosperity.

We find, where the ancient ideal has been maintained with dignity, that a benevolent autocracy on the part of elders, and unquestioning submission on the part of the younger members of the group, have made its realization possible and actual. "The Hindu youth has to maintain an attitude of utter indifference about every proposal regarding his marriage, and when any arrangement in that respect is made

[1] I am told that, especially in East Bengal, some Brāhman parents used to keep their daughters unwed rather than have them wives merely in name. They had a status similar to widows in the home.

by his parents, grandparents, uncles, or elder brothers, he has to go through the ceremony out of his sense of duty to obey or oblige them."[1]

This habit of submission to family authority in private life, and to the discipline of caste control in public relationships, has resulted in a law-abiding character which, in spite of latter-day upheavals due to various causes (usually far removed from the ostensible cause), is typical of the Hindu, and especially of the Bengali Hindu. The idea of *dharma*, or conformity to the ancient law, is, like the Roman *pietas*, very closely bound up with the details as well as the general spirit of man's daily life and conduct as a member of the family and caste group. As a rule, his duty is so clearly indicated by custom that he can be in no doubt about it. To be "correct" becomes his highest dharma. Any more passionate interpretation of the spiritual life cannot be attained within domestic circles, and involves the abandonment of *saṁsāra*—the normal life of the householder.

The head of the Bengali household is the oldest male member, the honour descending in the direct line. On his death, his son becomes the *karttā*, or master, even although his uncles may be alive and may be senior members of the same household. The honour is shared by his wife, who controls the feminine side of the household. She is known as the *grihinī*—not "mistress" but simply "housewife"—and is addressed by all members of the household, including the humblest menials, as *mā*—mother. The ideal house-mother fulfils this rôle very perfectly, treating servants like children with a homely kindness and "familiarity"—in the original sense of the word—which are admirable. But such a position also develops not infrequently an imperiousness of temper and hauteur of demeanour that can make others feel

[1] *Hindu Castes and Sects*, J. N. Bhattacharya, p. 340.

extremely "small." Imperiousness frequently shows itself in the smallest details. Not only is the will of the senior law, but his or her personal preferences rule the whole machinery of the household. This, of course, is often the case in Western households, but the constitution and customs of the Indian home make the autocratic temper an ever-present temptation to those in power.

Many of the household servants are men. In all large caste houses the cooks are a certain class of Brāhmans, familiarly known as *B'āhmanṭhākur*. The "bearers," many of whom come from Orissa, are of a more Dravidian type than the Bengali, and do the work of footmen and valets. "The washerwoman" is more usually a man, though his wife sometimes collects and brings back the clothes. Maidservants are employed in the scullery and as nurses for the younger children. Well-to-do women have waiting-maids, and, in poorer households, women instead of men are employed to help with cooking. Refuse is removed by the *Methars*, or sweeper class, who, because of their lowly work, are regarded as "untouchables." Or it may be more correct to say that, because they belong to a Pariah class, they are compelled to earn their living by the necessary work of scavenging and sanitation, which is in India carried out by most primitive methods.

It is at first surprising to a foreigner, who has heard of the strict seclusion of Bengali caste women, to discover the presence of men on the household staff, but one comes to understand that the designation of the chief housewife as mā has a special bearing on this matter. Manu says: "Beggars and working people may hold conversation with women."[1] The house servants are usually old family retainers, many of them having been born and brought up in

[1] *Manu*, viii. 360.

connection with the household. They are regarded as children of the house and are under the control of the senior women of the family. The young daughters-in-law are not supposed to have dealings with them, but a great part of the care of the children, especially outside of the house, is in the hands of these *chākars*, or serving men. At a pardā school for girls one sees them at the lunch hour feeding their little girl charges with milk and sweetmeats sent from home.

A Bengali woman is secluded from many of her male relatives, not eating even with her husband, and veiling her face before him if a third person is present. If his mother is standing by, she must not even address a remark to him. (No wonder the whole Orient thinks the Western woman hopelessly immodest!) But she is not secluded where servants are concerned, and this familiarity is almost never abused.

To understand Indian life, one must recognize the powerful "pull" that family exercises over individuals. There is no exact parallel to this in the English life of to-day. Perhaps in Eastern Europe family life is still more patriarchal than in the West, where only a faint ghost of the family, in the classical sense, survives. There is more "body" in the sentiment of family among the English land-owning classes, but, even in their case, younger sons and their progeny are apt to fade into obscurity. The sons in a Bengali family usually inherit an equal portion of their father's property, and it may be that this fact has been the cement in the structure of the *paribār* or group of relations. Together the sons could maintain their accustomed state by means of the common purse; separately they had to drop below their former prosperity. This was specially so when, as was most frequently the case, the property consisted of land.

Circumstances, such as joint responsibility for the land and a sharing of the family home, made a breaking up of the family almost impossible even if desired. In the present day many influences are combining to make disruption easy and almost unavoidable. The natural expansion of a family comes in time to lay too great a strain on its resources; the incurable tendency of the Indian to lavish display,[1] often shown in a hospitality far beyond his means at times when religious feasts, funeral ceremonies, weddings and other occasions demand entertainment of fellow-caste-men, the constant drain of marriage dowries, which is still one of the chief sources of impoverishment in Bengali families—all these factors make inevitable the drifting away of members of the family in search of careers to replenish their emptying coffers. Another fertile source of separations is the feuds, so apt to occur when a great many people are gathered under one roof.

The industrial expansion, due to the British occupation and to the establishment of larger relations with the rest of the world; the need for officers to carry on the administration; the opening up of professional careers in law, medicine, teaching, etc., have changed the poverty-stricken small landowner class into a bourgeois city population, which has not yet adapted itself comfortably to the new order of things. Posts befitting the sons of gentlemen are mobbed with applicants. The "church" and the army could not hitherto be numbered among these, as they were the special preserve of the Hindu priestly caste and the British officer. The army, however, is now to some extent open, and a few commissions are granted each year to suitable Indian candidates. Yet, in general, work suited to the tastes and prejudices of the upper classes being very limited and the number of candidates for all available posts rapidly

[1] Cf. Footnote, p. 78.

increasing in number, the bhadra-lok soon began to find the avenues of employment closed.

Within the last twenty years or so a change has come over the spirit of the Bengali bhadra-lok, and in a kind of desperation many of them are grasping at any sort of career open to men without capital. Entering into competition with the merchant class, who have trade in their blood and are too much for the gentlemanly amateur, well-bred Bengalis have suffered severe shocks and disillusionment in the marketplace, and pine for the simple life of the *sannyāsi*, or idle hanger-on in the security of the family home. "Sitting," the word used to describe the state of the unemployed, seems to point to a time when sitting in dignified idleness, being fanned by a hereditary retainer, was the proper state of a Bengali gentleman. The ideal, even of those who have been driven by the exigencies of the family fortunes to take *chākri*, i.e., service with Government or other employers less august, is to retire at the earliest possible moment on a pension sufficient to keep body and soul together, and to sit blissfully on the *gadi*, or mattress, of the sitting-room, barefoot and naked to the waist, while the pungent smoke of the hookah fills the air, and the bubbling sound of the water in its bowl makes an accompaniment infinitely soothing to memories of that strenuous and detestable life of bondage to another, now mercifully at an end.

Conduct in respect of family duty may certainly be described as "three-fourths of life" for the orthodox Hindu. For the Hindu woman it is four-fourths. Apart from her place in the family, she has in orthodox society no status, no place as an individual; while, under the ancestral roof she has protection, a clearly defined position and its corresponding prestige. Outside its walls she feels no safer than in a tiger-haunted jungle. The extent to which the sentiment of fear prevails in the minds of the women is shown by many instances. Recently an aged widow, who had herself lived a free and independent life for thirty years since adopting Christianity, pointed to her daughter and said: "At my death I wish her to be in your hands and under your protection." The daughter is a widow of about thirty years, and will on her mother's death inherit a considerable fortune. "As you know," her mother added, "no woman must live in our society by herself"—meaning Indian society in general.

That such fears are not ungrounded is proved by the fact that even refined and highly educated professional women, the product of modern higher education in India, have difficulty in retaining their reputation unblemished, so great are the hardships and temptations of their lot. This side of modern life is more fully discussed in the last chapter. Hardy and noble pioneers there have been who have braved severe trials to establish a new tradition: all honour to them. They have shown the spirit of the first voyagers in unknown seas or in the uncharted air, and in the future their names will be prized and their adventures extolled by those who in after years reap the fruit of their daring.

The emphasis in the patriarchal group is on the son and son's son. Woman's place is, therefore, of only relative importance. Her function is to make possible, by the bearing of sons, the unbroken carrying on of the sacred family tradition. It is difficult, impossible indeed, to reconcile the supreme importance attached by the Hindu to the birth of a son with the pessimism of the prevailing belief that existence is a curse and that salvation lies in *not* being born to the round of birth and death.

From childhood a woman's view is directed away from

her own patriarchal group, in which she has little part to play, to the possible family tree on which she may be grafted. This it is that makes the story of the marriage of Gaurī, the girl wife of the god Śiva, so popular and full of poignant meaning to the zenana woman. The period of a girl's connection with her father's house is made as brief as possible. Her life begins to have significance only when, at her marriage into another family,[1] she passes, or is passed rather, from the shelter of one roof-tree to the shelter of another. This passage takes places when she is little more than a child, and when unquestioning acceptance of the fiat of her parents is natural. It is counted a sacred obligation for a parent to hand over his daughter from his own guardianship at an age when her immaculate virginity cannot be called in question. A special traditional sanctity[2] attaches to the age of eight as a suitable one for marriage, Gaurī, Śiva's wife, according to general belief, having been married at that age. Popular songs, describing the event, and especially the sorrow of the bride's parents and the trembling fears of the child bride, have a universal appeal.[3]

Exceptions to the marriage of girls at an early age are now frequent, but the change is confined almost entirely to the reformed and well-to-do classes (still a small, though growing, section of society). The husband in these early marriages is not usually of an age to be considered the girl's guardian, being himself still under authority. The young girl goes from one obedience to another, from one

[1] *Short Stories*, by Kusika, gives striking pictures of Hindu marriage.

[2] A girl eight years old becomes a Gaurī, one of nine years a Rohinī, one of ten a Kanyā (maiden), after that Rajasvalā (a woman). *Samvarta Samhitā*, 66, Dutt's Translation, p. 341.

[3] *Bengali Religious Lyrics*, E. J. Thompson and A. M. Spencer, p. 26.

set of rules and duties to another; but of both her acceptance must be unquestioning. The little wife gains a new prestige when she becomes the mother of a son, and is addressed as *khokār mā*, "mother of the boy," by her household and the outside world. In section ix. of Manu's code, dealing with woman, verses 96 and 137, the belief in woman's destiny is plainly stated. "Women are created in order to bear children," and "Through a son one conquers worlds, through a son's son one attains endlessness, and through the son's son of a son one attains the world of the sun."

All this may appear to differ but slightly from universal views of the matter, but there *is* a difference. It is central in the minds of all, and the sonless mother regards herself as unblessed and as reaping the fruit of some evil *karma*.[1] Childlessness in the first wife justifies any Hindu in taking another wife.

In her new position of daughter-in-law the Bengali girl is left in no doubt as to her behaviour. She is a cog on the wheel, fitting into a system almost mechanical in its precision, the *āchāra vyavahāra*, or manners and customs, which have the force of a religious code. Her forms of politeness follow a rule of rigid propriety, according to which each senior member of the household has rights and honours which must duly be recognized, and particular designations to be used instead of personal names, some of which, if translated literally, would seem almost like titles for the gods. Only in the case of those younger than herself may she use names.

Strict precedence defines her own place in the family. If

[1] Karma, the Hindu doctrine of the fruit of action whereby the deeds of one existence create the conditions of the next, or even create the next existence.

she is the first wife of her generation, she has an importance second only to her mother-in-law, but quite subordinate as long as the latter is able to exercise control. In her early days as a wife she is without authority and almost without responsibility in her husband's house, except in trifling matters. Even the care of her babies is sometimes taken over by older women. An older woman, nursing an infant, pointed to the mother of the baby, playing with a doll, and remarked rather sarcastically to me, "The child prefers her dolls." The young wife is, as a rule, silent, discreet and timid in outward bearing, and a model of polite docility, at least in all households with pretensions to good manners. Conformity to a recognized standard is what is enjoined on her and expected of her from infancy.

The extraordinary passivity of the Indian girl is expressed with a good deal of pathos, not untouched with cynicism, in one of the *Tales of Bengal*, by the sisters Chatterjee. A mother and daughter are described, the scene being a train bound for Calcutta, whither they are travelling in search of a husband. The mother is garrulous and informs her fellow-passengers of her affairs. "Indeed, it is only to the greatest of sinners that daughters are born," she remarks. She bemoans her daughter's dark complexion, which makes it impossible to get a bridegroom without giving a great dowry. Then we are told of the girl: "There was no pained look in her eyes, nor tears, nor did her heart respond to the cruel words of her mother in painful throbs, for such heartlessness was her daily food, and her mind had long become dead to such insults. So nobody could have judged from her appearance that she herself was the object of these heartless words."[1] Further on, when the young girl's face has been exhibited to the

[1] *Tales of Bengal*, p. 8.

other passsengers in proof of her mother's ill-luck, the story continues: "Her aged daughter at once assumed her former position and remained still like a stranded boat"—a phrase revealing poetic insight into the girl mind of Bengal.

In a book for young wives in the vernacular, entitled *Gāye Halud*[1] (the smearing of the body with turmeric paste, customary among the women at marriage ceremonies), which contains advice to the newly married girl, the following words occur (in rough translation): "No matter what is being said about you, you must behave like a *Siddha-purusha* (holy man). You must not give any sign of being hurt or annoyed. You should not even smile at the remarks. You must keep your eyes fixed on the ground." This refers to insulting comments on the newly-arrived bride's appearance by the village gossips, made in the girl's presence. "Be like a picture or a doll. If you can maintain that attitude, you will win the name of Lakshmī, daughter-in-law." (Lakshmī is a goddess, and the name is used colloquially to mean "model.") This advice is given in all seriousness. "You are a new daughter-in-law. Society does not permit you to speak."

It is often said that behind the pardā the power of woman is supreme. But this, in so far as it is true, applies chiefly to women who happen to be heads of households. In any large family house these will be few in number, and there will always be several others who have never had, and may never have, any real power at all. They will never become mistress of a house as we understand the word. The exercise of a wife's powers may be restricted to the control of her own children and a certain influence over her husband, if he is susceptible to her persuasions. In folk-tales woman is often shown as advising her husband

[1] D. C. Sen, p. 28.

to certain courses, and is usually portrayed as possessing more common sense than the man, who, especially if he is a Brāhman, is made to appear as a very gullible and unpractical person. Yet, on the other hand, there is a common saying, *Strībuddhi pralayaṅkarī*—"Woman's wisdom brings doom."

Often a husband is so placed that for fear of his mother he must act as though his wife's opinion were of little account,[1] and the wife has to exercise a good deal of diplomacy because of the fear that, if she falls out of favour with husband or mother-in-law, she may be superseded.

Thus it frequently happens that a woman never, even in her old age, enjoys any recognized authority, since her husband may never become head of the house. It is curious to observe the docility of gray-headed "juniors" in a large household. They never lose a certain childishness of demeanour. A Bengali lady known to the writer, who had lived in strict pardā till the age of fifty or so used to say: "When my mother-in-law dies, all shall be changed. My husband says so." And it was: the shrinking pardānaśin became thoroughly Western in her style of living, and a leader in the new reformed Hindu society of Calcutta. But by that time she was too old to enjoy her strange freedom. It irked her.

It is little wonder that Indians sometimes appear unable or unwilling to think for themselves in practical matters, and expect and prefer to be told what to do by some one recognized as having the right to command.

Thus "set in families," the Bengali woman has little acquaintance with the idea expressed in that blessed word "self-determination." Her life is determined from without, and not from within her own mind, just as physically, it is

[1] *Vide infra*, p. 82.

circumscribed by the four walls of her home. The walls that stand round her mind are the will of her mother-in-law, the will of her husband, and, in old age, the will of her son, unless, as not uncommonly happens in India, she has exceptional strength of character and gains a powerful influence over him. It is indeed the true sphere of woman's vaunted influence. An Indian writer says: "One might almost say that the native States are ruled by the queen mothers from behind the pardā," and this, in spite of the fact that one of the most often-quoted sayings of Manu is: "Let a woman never enjoy independence, but be under authority of father, husband, son."

The "blessed" word for woman is *usage*. In Manu, i. 108, are the words: "Usage is highest dharma (it is) mentioned in the Vedas, and approved by tradition, therefore a prudent, twice-born (man) shall ever be intent on this." One might almost say that for the women custom is religion and religion custom, "The scrupulous ways of the religion of the hearth . . ." according to Pater, a "religion of usages and sentiment rather than of facts and beliefs."[1]

We speak of the *accident* of birth. There is nothing accidental, to the Hindu mind, in the birth or circumstances of any man or woman. He or she is born precisely in a certain caste or family, because of deeds committed in previous existences. It is inevitable that a thorough-going belief in fate, such as is almost universal among Hindus, should bring into thought and action a rigidity that is foreign to the genius of freer races, and maintain customs, fashions and even ideas unchanged through hundreds of years. "In the path by which one's father walked, by which one's grandparents walked, by that one should

[1] *Marius the Epicurean*, Walter Pater, vol. i. p. 4.

go the way of the good."[1] This saying of Manu still seems to the majority in India the safest rule of life. To break through customs so hoary becomes an act of fearful impiety and sacrilege. Few individuals have the courage to take such risks of unhappiness.

Hospitality on the occasion of festivals, domestic and religious, is a duty which the Hindu house-mother fulfils not perfunctorily, but with a grace and readiness that are altogether admirable. Dr. Samuel Johnson, in a letter to Mrs. Thrale, describes charmingly the hospitality of the Hebrides. "The guest is received," he says, "as if he had come to confer a benefit." No words could be more apt as a description of the cordial manner of the Hindu lady in her own house. She radiates kindliness and, although shy and nervous at times, never fails in giving an unmistakable welcome; for she looks upon it as a duty truly religious to do her utmost for the provision and comfort of her guests. Her entertainment meets the demand of St. Paul, "*pursue* hospitality" and that "without grudging." A Tamil poet thus voices this Indian ideal: "The wife is she who, although want is in the house, when relations come to feast enough to drain an ocean, gently welcomes all and shines like the goddess of the house."[2] Relations very often do come in battalions. One person to whom it is politic as well as kind to show special hospitality is the son-in-law. Nothing is too good to set before him. Yet, curiously enough, no woman cares to take hospitality from her daughter's husband nor to stay under his roof.

[1] *Manu*, iv. 178.

[2] Quoted in *Indian Thought, Past and Present*, R. W. Frazer, p. 305.

CHAPTER IV

THE BENGALI WOMAN

Grihastha bārir meye (Daughter of a household) is the usual description of a respectable Hindu woman in Bengal. The designation at once gives her status and title to honour; so it is in the midst of her family life that we may best observe her and consider her characteristics; and although no view of the present day can afford to ignore the "new woman" in Bengal and elsewhere in India, the point of view from which Bengali women in general may be studied is expressed by a French writer as follows: "A man exists only in relation to his surroundings which he has fashioned, and which help to fashion him, or, at least, to keep him true to himself."[1]

To be greeted by a Bengali woman of the secluded classes on the threshold of her home, is to become aware immediately that India has treasures which she does not display to the common eye, and that here we have found something fine and rare. Her winsome and dignified manner reveals a personality that possesses "quality." And such quality can only be the fruit of a civilization and social culture not yet, perhaps, wholly understood or appreciated by the European. The European cannot be blamed for this lack of understanding, because it is in large measure

[1] *Three Studies in English Literature*, André Chevrillon.

due to the very fact of the seclusion of Indian women. This seclusion has resulted, among other things, in a great part, and that the better part, of the life of the people being hidden from the foreigner.

"Babudom," to give it an uneuphonious name, the world of Hindu employees familiar to the average European, is one thing, and the Hindu home, where the "babu" is host and master, is another and very different affair. When the foreigner is admitted into the Hindu home, he finds himself in an environment which is unfamiliar and often quite unknown to the average European. The chief cause of this difference is the presence of the women, who hold sway in the home. Insight into real family life is only afforded on rare occasions; for most of the entertainment of Europeans in Indian houses is formal and ceremonious, and the women take no part in it.

A similar ignorance of the Englishman's home makes "sahibdom" the only aspect of the European known to "babudom." A Brāhman doctor, who by some unusual circumstance became for some time an inmate of an English doctor's home in India, was astonished at the motherliness of the doctor's wife, her punctilious attention to his personal comfort, her devotion to the care of her children, and her daily personal supervision of her house and servants in the matter of food and cleanliness. Such painstaking efficiency and motherly ways were a revelation to him. Having asked permission to follow her through her morning routine, he exclaimed at last: "No Indian house that I know of is kept like yours. It is wonderful." He had previously, no doubt, accepted the fiction current in India, that the Englishwoman is no housewife, and is at best frivolous and pleasure-loving and at worst prone to abuse her liberty on the slightest opportunity. Many Indians hold the belief very firmly that all but the modicum of education unfits a woman for domesticity.

This unfamiliarity of one race with the intimate life of the other has bred much mutual misunderstanding and even mutual contempt. Only a small section of Europeans can be in a position to judge whether the following attempt to draw a picture of the Bengali pardānaśin is successful, or not.

The Bengali woman has a goodly share of natural beauty. In figure and feature she stands comparison with the finest races of the world. The average height is not great, but the graceful proportions of her frame prevent any impression of insignificance on account of her stature. In complexion she is of fairer colour than the southern and western races of India, but darker than the northern. Often within one family and caste one finds different degrees of colour. Under favourable conditions her skin is smooth and clear. Even when her colouring is not of the fairest, the lustre and expressiveness of her fine eyes, and the beauty of white and even teeth light up her face. The features are refined and sometimes of a classical regularity, and, in families where a careful selection of good-looking brides has perfected the type, one sees occasionally young women of rare and fascinating beauty.

Her hair is plentiful, sometimes to an extent one had thought of as legendary, falling, when unbound, like a cloak to her ankles. It is glossy and of a blue-black hue, and its natural sheen is heightened by the constant application of oil and by frequent exposure to the rays of the sun. Natural curls are common enough, but are not encouraged, as it is a sign of dignity and modesty to have smoothly braided locks. On special occasions this braiding is done in intricate designs.

Photographs by Edna Lorenz.

BENGALI HIGH CASTE LADY—A WIDOW.

The daily bath, which is a habit with the Hindus of Bengal, is accompanied by the pouring of water on the head. The water cools the scalp, but runs off the well-oiled hair. In order to dry the head, the hair is worn loose in the morning and often dried in the sun. The wealth of hair is concealed by this daily moistening; it is only when it has been washed in a lather of soap-nut or some other alkaline substance, and freed from oil, that one has a chance of seeing its magnificence. In the country the poorer women use mud as a hair cleanser—with what results I have had no opportunity of observing. Lentil flour is also used for the same purpose.

Before marriage, a girl wears her hair drawn tightly back from the forehead, and arranged in a plaited coil flat against the back of the head and kept in place by silver pins. More elaborate coiffures are made with beaded nets and gold-plated combs. "Full dress," such as a bride's, includes a great variety of head ornaments made of gold and gems, the bridal coronet being particularly rich. After marriage, the hair is parted in the middle, and just above the forehead is placed the vermilion mark, signifying the wedded state. It is a sign of the times that Christian women, who had discarded this headmark in favour of the wedding ring, have begun to use it again, along with the Christian symbol, as being a national custom. In widowhood the hair is either neglected and undressed, or, more frequently, shaved altogether. The object of this sign of mourning may be that the glory of woman shall no longer form an attraction to the other sex.

At every stage of a woman's life the manner of wearing her hair has special significance. The old-fashioned, demure style of hairdressing suits the Bengali type of face, with its finely marked eyebrows and brilliant eyes. A more "fluffy" mode of arranging the hair, now in vogue among young women students and others, seems to rob them of some of their natural and distinguishing charm.

The ideal of feminine beauty, according to Bengali standards, demands what they describe as "golden" or "rose-coloured" skin—meaning the creamy colour of the tea rose, and not what we usually mean by rosy. The face should be oval with straight and delicate features, eyes of an almond shape, slightly tilted upwards at the outer corners, with long lashes and finely arched brows, red lips and small even teeth. A girl must not be too tall: about five feet is a favourite height; her figure should be slight and lissom, but perfectly rounded, even to "chubbiness," the hands small, plump and dimpled, the feet also rather plump, so that the bones do not show, and shapely, but not too highly arched—this being an unfavourable omen. Great attention is paid to the feet by fastidious women. The hereditary barber's wife is usually an expert at manicure and pedicure, and pays regular visits to women of good family.

The feet being untrammelled from childhood, are usually delicate in shape and expressive of refinement. Children at school pick up pencils, and even needles, very deftly with their toes, and often express embarrassment by curling and uncurling them, as we might do our fingers.

The expression of a Bengali girl's face ought, to satisfy ideas of charm, to be winsome but modest withal, and her bodily movements soft and slow but not heavy. The dignified gait of a well-bred woman is often compared to an elephant's walk. To us this may appear a ludicrous comparison; but when one has seen the majestic yet placid motion of a richly caparisoned elephant in a state procession, one begins to understand the simile.

Too much vivacity, "bounce," and impulsiveness, are

considered unbecoming even in a young maiden, and more so in a wife. This standard of quietness is as old as Manu, who says: "One should not be restless with hands and feet, or restless with the eyes." Sometimes the excessive curbing of the natural effervescence of girlhood results in an almost cow-like passivity; and the lack of vigorous motion causes women to grow too stout at an early age. This stoutness, which is very common, and is, no doubt, in part due to climate and diet as well as to the inactive life of the zenana, often changes beautiful girls into plain-looking women. But among Bengalis it is not considered altogether unbecoming in adults to be stout. The modern tennis-playing Indian lady may lose some of the respect of her community, but she preserves her youthful charms much longer than her secluded sister.

The Bengali woman of the bhadra class has attractive and very natural manners, and she possesses the repose which we associate with good breeding. Although shy, she is seldom gauche or ill at ease, even in unusual circumstances. In consequence, she has the power of setting others at their ease, and intercourse with her is cordial and agreeable. Her seclusion from the world has preserved in her a certain girlish artlessness which is very winning, and a first encounter with her is like conversing with a frank and eager child rather than with a sophisticated "grown-up."

Trained in the polite reception of guests, the pardā lady would be courteous in any case, but to a European who has taken the trouble to visit her in her home, she gives credit for genuine goodwill, and makes a warm-hearted response to the visitor's overtures. Friendly callers are too rare to be a mere convention, much less a bore, and she is ready at once to lay aside whatever she may be busied with, or rise from her siesta without any grudge. The only occupation which she will not interrupt for a visitor is eating, if she has actually sat down to a meal. The caller must wait until that is finished, or come later. A widow must not leave her meal in the middle.

No doubt this is due to the cooking arrangements. It is not easy to make Indian food palatable again if it has been left to get cold, and there is also the caste prejudice against "left" food, which is regarded as unclean. No one will eat "leavings" in India except the Pariah. Food left unguarded might become contaminated. Yet in another connection, which will be referred to in dealing with the Hindu woman's religion, it will be noticed that left food is sometimes sacred.[1] Low castes think it a privilege to eat the leavings of Brāhmans.

The visitor, having been received, is treated with kindly consideration. If the heat or flies are troublesome, her hostess will ply a fan unwearyingly, inquire anxiously if the guest is comfortable, and offer sweetmeats if it is a first visit. It is considered desirable, both for the honour of the house and the pleasure of the guest, that she should depart "with a sweet mouth." If sweets are refused by the guest, spices are offered in the form of *pān supāri*[2] or simply cloves, cardamums, cinnamon-stick, etc., so that one often nibbles these as one carries on conversation. Finally, the hostess speeds the parting guest with the gracious word "Come." This word is also tactfully used to indicate dismissal when necessary—meaning, go now, but come at some more convenient season.

Those who enjoy this simple, happy intercourse, and experience the pleasure of feeling truly welcome, cannot

[1] *Vide infra*, p. 110.

[2] Chopped nut wrapped in aromatic leaf.

help asking: Whence comes this air of cheerful tranquillity, and how can it be that women, who have so few of the privileges and opportunities which those of other lands count as their right, have still so much to give of the things that cannot be weighed or defined? The chance visitor to a Bengali home has the sense of having discovered a true source of pleasure and enrichment. This has been the writer's own impression, and others who have been introduced to the world behind the pardā, have expressed themselves as deeply interested and attracted by their glimpse of a hitherto unknown region.

The Bengali pardā woman is ready to be pleased with any interruption in the monotony of her daily round. A certain eagerness is shown in receiving a messenger from outside, more sophisticated than herself and more closely in touch with the realities of the world which she only knows by hearsay.

Conversation on a first acquaintance with a Hindu household is apt to consist of a fire of questions. It is not considered impolite to inquire of the visitor how old she is, whether she is married or not, how many children she has, what are her husband's occupation and income, what she is in the habit of eating, the size of her house and number of her servants, the country of her birth and the position there of her father and father-in-law. These topics are here enumerated in detail, because in almost every house all of them are subjects of intense curiosity.

While some of the group listen to the answers to these queries, others, with that almost uncanny insight which is characteristic of Indians generally, are drawing their own conclusions from the visitor's person, manners, clothes and ornaments, and deciding, with astonishing accuracy, her birth, class, upbringing and character. They give expression to the opinions thus formed among themselves, and the visitor cocks her ears to catch the general drift of their remarks amidst the babel of chatter, while she either answers or waves aside as irrelevant a further instalment of questions, such as:

"Do you put oil on your hair?"

"Do you eat rice every day, or 'foot' bread?" This refers to the rather unpleasant legend that bakers' loaves are kneaded with the feet.

"Are your feet white like your face?" This question is sometimes accompanied by a request to remove shoes and stockings.

"Why do you wear one bracelet instead of a pair, and why are your ears not pierced for ear-rings, which would be so becoming?"

Our lack of jewellery mystifies them, and gives rise to grave doubts as to the affection of husband and relatives-in-law. It takes a good deal of explaining to persuade them that it is all right, and just another of our unaccountable peculiarities that we think much jewellery unsuitable for wearing with our style of dress. Their questions about European babies reveal strange streaks of ignorance.

"Are your babies born fair, or is their skin treated at birth by some bleaching process?"

"Is it true that they are bathed in brandy as soon as they are born, and that that is what makes your race white?"

"Do their mothers suckle them?" This they find hard to believe, because it is not done publicly and because babies' bottles are a Western invention.

The writer was once urgently entreated by an old woman to tell her the great secret of our bleaching process. She had several granddaughters-in-law to whom she was greatly attached, but not one of whom was fair, and she wished to "improve" their appearance. Her disappointment, when I assured her that there was no such secret, was pathetic to witness, and I suppose she thought I was sworn not to reveal it. Sometimes one hears the remark made humorously: "Let the matter alone. We have dark skins because we have black hearts. In another birth with better hearts, we shall have better complexions." Frequently, when the writer has admired a baby, the mother has remarked: "What? can you see any beauty in a dark-skinned child?" This is partly an instance of that tendency to say flattering things, which is considered good manners in India, but, taking all these references together, one is astonished to find so much insistence upon the colour aspect of races. It is my only excuse for referring to it, knowing that it is a subject that bristles with possibilities of misunderstanding.

From what one hears of this matter one is driven to the conclusion that the people of India imagine that the European is always conscious of the colour of his own skin, and they can hardly be persuaded that he rarely gives the matter a thought. They also seem to believe that the European bases a claim to superiority on this ground alone. This idea seems to be an echo of very ancient struggles between different races and cultures broadly distinguished by colour differences, of which one phase was the struggle between Aryans and aborigines, a struggle resembling that of the Jews and Canaanites in the Land of Promise. The ancient name for caste, *varṇa*, means colour, and seems to point to a ranging of races according to degrees of fairness.

The mixed races of India, jealous of their relation to the ruling race, are apt to emphasise this difference in a somewhat offensive way. Bengalis are, for some reason, hyper-sensitive on this point, and frequently, as has been shown above, drag the subject into conversation, as if they almost enjoyed being hurt by brooding over it and imagining contempt where none is felt. When one hears a "sahib" speaking of Indians as "black people," it is almost a certain proof that the speaker is of mixed blood; and one most frequently hears this kind of talk from those who, in vulgar idiom, are perhaps only "two annas in the rupee" European.

A curious practice of posing as injured by you, the injurer, who should, in consequence, be uncomfortably stirred by compunction and solicitude towards the victim of your alleged unkindness, is often noticeable in Bengali girls and women—and men too. They admit this trait themselves, and say: "We are a very *abhimānī*, i.e. 'touchy,' race." I have known a girl use many devices to engineer herself, and the person whose favour she craves, into the mutual relation of wounded and wounder. This is not an uncommon weakness of human nature, but it almost amounts to a fine art among Bengalis of the more emotional type, a type which predominates among them. They are past masters at putting you in the wrong, and unless you are on your guard against this peculiar power, you will come to have a very low opinion of yourself, and imagine that you really are incapable of justice—that is, if it is your lot to be closely associated with them in work and in daily life. Along with this goes an inability to admit themselves in the wrong and a tendency to self-pity. "So-and-so has done me a great injustice," is a plaint often heard in the land.

In contrast to this type is that, more frequently found among the more independent races, of the person too proud to let you discover that you have it in your power to injure him. It is difficult to decide which kind of pride is less desirable.

It is natural that among Indian women special curiosity should be displayed about everything connected with marriage customs, this being, in their own lives, the matter above all that affects their destiny. One is interested to note that, even where our customs differ most widely from theirs, as in the possibility of free choice of husband or wife, and the re-marriage of widows, and where these differences puzzle and perhaps even shock them, they still admit that they are right for *us*, since these are the customs of our *samāj* or society. Even spinsterhood, which puts their faith in us to a severe test, becomes acceptable, because, strange and unnatural though it be, it is still our *niyam* or rule.

This apparent catholicity of judgment, which surprises one at first by its breadth, becomes, as one learns to understand more clearly their views on conduct, merely another sign of their belief in the rigid adherence of each section of society to its own conventions. Actions are not right or wrong in their nature, but only as they conform, or fail to conform, to a standard of propriety set up by general consent: "That which is permitted." Woman's part in Asiatic countries has been to "toe the line" and ask no questions. It is amusing to note how the air of pained surprise which at first greets the confirmation of the tale they have heard—that it is not unusual for our widows to marry again—often gives way to a protest from some shrewd member of the company that it is a very good thing too, and that she wishes their widows were as lucky.

The Bengali woman is a ready talker, quick, lively, and often witty, with a keen eye for human foibles. To be hilarious is not considered "good form," and there is often a studied dignity, and, in company at least, a restraint almost too great in the manner of a well-bred woman. In the early years of married life a girl is expected to observe silence in the presence of her seniors, unless directly addressed, but, away from them, and with others of her own age, she can be merry enough and delights in banter and repartee. Their wit is more caustic than good-humoured, and their "chaff" apt to be too heavy-handed. They are capable of playfulness, but the depressing influence of climate tends to make sobriety more habitual.

Sometimes banter takes a curiously conventional form like the moves in a well-known game. There are certain sayings and gestures always calculated to produce the same effect of amusement, or mild exasperation, or real annoyance. Especially is this so when a quarrel takes place. The same time-worn terms of contempt and abuse are hurled at one's opponent: "burnt-faced," "destroyer of salt," "destroyer of good fortune," and so on. It is like a formula learnt by heart, and in the excitement of passion can be uttered with the speed and vehemence of a cataract, so rapid and ceaseless is the torrent of words, the voice rising and being sustained on a high, shrill note which makes it penetrate to a long distance. A Hindu who supplied the writer with a list of these verbal weapons, when asked if he himself ever used such terms, replied cheerfully: "Why, yes, to my wife and daughter when they annoy me." A woman draws the line at the choice of terms, of which there is a considerable variety, and at the degree of fury displayed, according to her breeding and natural refinement; but the impropriety of flying into a rage and "brawling" is not felt very acutely even by women of good family.

In the course of a family jar at which the writer was an unseen and unwilling spectator, one of the women, a lady by class and education, when words had failed her, seized her shoe and struck a male member of the house on the forehead. Insult could go no further, for even to shake your shoe at anyone is a supreme sign of contempt. The reaction upon the woman, horrified as she was at herself, took the form of a reiterated sobbing protest: "I am glad I did it. I am glad I did it." On another occasion there was a display of temper on the part of one of the guests at a wedding. Shouting continuously at the top of his voice, regardless of the trembling bride and shamefaced bridegroom, he marched out of the house with all his party. A Bengali, who was present with the writer, said smilingly: "Oh, that is quite usual. My grandfather smashed all the chandeliers at his son's wedding, because he considered that the bride's father had not shown him sufficient respect."

One's experience is confirmed by modern stories of domestic life. In *Tales of Bengal*, a collection of short stories by the sisters Chatterjee, we read: "There were the same brutal shouts from the bridegroom's party, the same abject entreaties from the bride's relations, and the very same wails from the women's apartments. The next instant I remembered that such a scene was not, after all, of rare occurrence in Bengal."[1] The same writers say: "A Hindu woman has at times to suffer torments that would beat the records of hell."[2] If this is indeed so, one cannot wonder that a want of self-control is so often apparent. In *The Home and the World*, a novel of Bengali home life under modern conditions, Dr. Tagore

[1] *Tales of Bengal*, p. 84. [2] *Tales of Bengal*, p. 105.

speaks of "The slime of domestic life that lay below the lotus bank of womanhood."

The instability of temper is partly due to climate. The European in India is all too conscious of this in himself, and has to fight against a tendency to depression, irritation, and, it may be, fury. One has heard of medical men applying the name "tropical fury" to a certain chronic state of irritability following upon Indian fevers and other maladies. It may be that the conventional expletives used by Bengalis are a provision designed to act as a safety valve when a nerve storm threatens an explosion.

The monotony and confinement of the women's lives often result in a lack of nerve control which shows itself in various forms of hysteria. The prevailing tendency to "fits" of despondency, anger, jealousy and sulks makes one wonder if these are not natural to womenkind even of normal constitution, and are only held in check, as among Englishwomen, by a strong public sentiment of disapproval and an early training that treats "tantrums" of every sort as a punishable offence. The extraordinary paroxysms of anger exhibited among the Bengalis by very young children and even infants, whom one has seen making their bodies stiff with rage, are not sufficiently checked, and, as a result, loss of control becomes a habit at an early stage, and has very mischievous effects later in life.

The love of Indian mothers for their children, beginning as it does so often in the years of girlhood, is apt to be doting and partial. They love their own children passionately, but the love does not always include the other children of the house. This is a fertile source of domestic quarrels.

They cannot understand how English mothers in India can be so callous as to send their children away to England,

and even when it is explained to them that it is for the children's good, they say a little unctuously, "We could not do it, we love our children too much. Your love is not like ours." Children thus loved become little tyrants. I have seen a sturdy boy of four years raining blows upon his mother's breast because she tried to resist his demand to be suckled. Usually in the end she gives in to his tyranny, little dreaming how by so doing she lays the seeds of future trouble for herself and him. Women tend to take meekly the rôle of victims to the caprices of others—their own children especially—and although I have seen a mother shake or slap her child with the passion of another angry child, it is considered unmotherly for a woman to smack her child deliberately for naughtiness. Such punishment, if administered by anyone, is taken as a great personal affront by a child, and many a small girl has left school in high dudgeon because of some slight slap from an impatient teacher, which she describles as "beating."

The prolonged strain of early marriage and maternity is sufficient to account for much of the alternating passivity and excitability of the pardānaśin. Besides these physical tests she has, while still young and sensitive, to pass through the ordeal of adapting herself to persons and ways that are strange to her. The relief which we find in outdoor exercise, variety of scene, and even casual social intercourse, are debarred from her, hence the eager interest shown when a visitor appears. Just two hours before these words were written the writer was visiting a Brāhman widow, who said wistfully, with tears rolling down her cheeks: "It is so long since you, or any of my old teachers, have been to see me, and it has been so dull day after day with no one to talk to. I cannot get away from the unhappiness in my heart." The wonder is, not that the Bengali pardā women are hysterical at times but that, in the main, they are patient, sweet-tempered, and even contented with their lot.

In spite of the lack of literary education, many of the women in all classes of Bengali society show a great natural intelligence and interest in ideas. Talk on general topics calls forth a quick response, and sometimes very shrewd criticism. Left to themselves, a company of illiterate Bengali women might be content to keep the conversation at a very low level of triviality, but that is because so many of their daily concerns are petty; yet it is true that they are often conscious of mental powers which have no proper exercise. "My desire for knowledge nearly drives me mad," said one to the writer; and another, who ran away from her husband, gave as her reason: "They do not understand me there. It is not that I want to break caste or change my religion, but I want to learn and learn and learn."

The small number of Bengali women who have been educated have shown their mettle and proved their capacity for intellectual cultivation. A race that has produced women like Mrs. Sarajini Naidu and Toru Dutt has no need to apologise for the intellectual quality of its women; but it has much need to bow its head in shame for the way in which it has starved keen and hungry minds. A writer in *The London Quarterly Review*[1] some years ago said: "Had Toru Dutt been a Hindu" (she was of Christian parentage), "the burdens of premature wifehood, probably of premature motherhood, would have made her story impossible. As regards its girls the Bengali people loses at least five years of childhood, and the loss is one for which nothing

[1] E. J. Thompson, in an article subsequently included in *The Life and Letters of Toru Dutt.*

can offer any shadow of compensation. When I made this comment to Bengal's greatest poet, he replied: 'I quite agree with you, and it is the saddest thing in our lives. . . . And first, of all the things that must be done and sought, this elementary justice must be rendered, and woman be free to expand and find herself. Then Toru Dutt, in her greatness of soul and her greatness of mind, will no more be a solitary and astounding phenomenon, but the firstborn star in a heaven of many lights.'"

The emergence in public life of outstanding personalities among Bengali women is rare because of the environment of women generally. At a very early age they find themselves in a position in which their happiness depends on their docility and submissiveness to their new relatives. Respect for the mother-in-law and complaisance of temper have been the chief articles in all they have been taught. Just as they are trained physically to a noiseless gait so that their coming and going in the house shall be as gentle as the fall of a leaf, so, mentally, they are broken into a habit of unobtrusiveness. "Individuality does not command, and never has commanded, such respect in India as it does in the West. Self-suppression, not self-expression or self-development, is still, as it has always been, the highest ideal of the best Indian minds. . . . Individual initiative, in which the Western world puts its trust, is in India restrained by a multitude of inhibitions."[1]

A certain place and part in life are assigned to woman in India, and she has been shaped and disciplined to that end. Before deciding on any course of action she has to consult the wishes and prejudices of a whole host of relatives, and

[1] Ramsay Muir, in Introduction to *Indian Nationality*, by R. N. Gilchrist.

her own impulses are often paralysed by their opposition, for which she may be able to see no good reason.

When a Western woman says: "I know my duty," she usually means that, after reflection, she has resolved to carry out a purpose which, according to her conviction, is right. Duty for an Indian woman, as has been indicated, is not so much a matter of personal conviction based on a principle of innate rightness as merely a recognized rule or custom. "Who am I, that I should go against the general custom?" is a remark often heard, and one which betrays the all but universal attitude of conservatism.

To quote Dr. Tagore's novel again: "Has not the pressure of society cramped them into pettiness and crookedness? They are but pawns of the fate which gambles with them. What responsibility have they of their own?"[1] The question relates to the woman of the upper classes in Bengal at the beginning of the twentieth century. Even since the words were written, however, some attempt has been made to give municipal and political responsibility to women in some of the provinces.[2]

To this view of duty may be traced the Bengali mother's idea of the education proper for girls. Education does not mean for her the development of the mental faculties, such as reason, imagination, judgment, inventiveness; but, on the contrary, a training of the will to submissivness and unquestioning acceptance of authority. Initiative comes to be regarded as an impertinence. This idea shows itself all through Indian life. If you remonstrate with your cook for

[1] *The Home and the World*, p. 10.

[2] A Bengali reader, Mr. J. N. C. Ganguly, made the remark on this statement that the apparent civic and political freedom was largely nullified by the lack of social freedom. Women are so placed that they cannot exercise the larger freedom.

ĀLPANĀ.

From the painting by J. Seal.

'Ālpanā' is the name given to a mode of decorating the floor which is traditional among the women of Bengal. The designs are drawn with powdered rice and water, producing an effect like that of white paint, but easily removed, and the elements of the pattern are varied by custom according to the festival that is being celebrated. Thus plaintain shoots and mango leaves, being associated with spring, are used in designs for weddings, first-rice, initiation, etc., to symbolize prosperity, an ear of paddy may be used for Lakshmi Puja, and the lotus for the most gorgeous festival of the year, the Durga Puja. The pattern is designed to suit the occasion, e.g. to adorn the standing-place for the newly wedded couple, or to provide a place of dignity for the idol to be worshipped.

getting into a rut and always giving the same dishes, he replies with an air of injury, " Have I not always given what the Huzoor commanded ? "

One observes how, among Bengali women, the powers of invention and initiative natural to the human mind became atrophied for want of exercise. The compulsion from without, which is brought to bear upon them at every point implicitly or explicitly, gradually robs them of the power and even the desire of free choice. If a girl is handed about as a chattel when she is too young to protest, but not too young to feel the pangs of separation from the guardians and companions of her childhood; if the functions of wife and mother are ruthlessly demanded of her, when these are not only not voluntarily or gladly exercised, but are a source of fear, and sometimes of acute distress and agony to her, there assuredly takes place a slow but certain damaging of those precious elements of human personality which in truly free peoples flower in strongly marked character and power, both in the individual and the race. If the people of Bengal are lacking in certain of the stronger traits, may it not be because they have heedlessly destroyed these qualities at the springs, in robbing their innocent girls of what should be voluntarily given and never forcibly taken. As long as defencelessness is exploited, as it is in Bengal, so long will society suffer from paralysis and unhappiness.

One finds the Bengali woman, outwardly at least, meek and self-effacing, timid and polite. The influences of her life have not tended, it is true, to develop the stronger virtues of self-reliance, courage, and self-control; but, on the other hand, they have brought into prominence some of the more passive virtues, sometimes in a superb degree.

In some respects the Indian woman is peerless, and one would deprecate any change, if such change threatened to diminish her distinguishing graces. Her repose and dignity, quiet, seemly bearing and sweetness of manner, and the simplicity of her household ways, make her winsome and loveable. But although her manners are much to be admired, and although manners are a part of character, they are not the whole of character nor can they ever be a substitute for character.

One result of her position of subordination frequently noticeable is a lack of serious purpose in her life. She drifts along. Other results, all too evident, are an inability to realize the value of time (an extraordinary amount of time is wasted, according to our notions, in the East), a want of the sense of proportion, lack of fearless rectitude, too much diplomacy, too much intrigue, too much tendency to sacrifice principle in order to gain some private end and win favour with the powers that be, and an absorbing interest in much that is excessively trivial regarding food, personal adornment, and the tittle-tattle and incessant bickerings of a large household. These are indeed the very faults to which woman everywhere is proverbially prone, but they are exaggerated in the life of the pardānaśin, who cannot breathe the larger air which clears the mind and brain of pettiness.

The heroine of *The Home and the World* thus soliloquizes: "Once I remember, in defence of some untruth of mine I said to my husband: 'Only the trees and beasts and birds tell unmitigated truths because the poor things have not the power to invent . . . neither is a profusion of ornament unbecoming for a woman nor a profusion of untruth.'" This generally accepted standard is evidently an ancient and time honoured one. Manu says: "One man (alone) may be a witness . . . but not even several women, although they may be pure, on account of the lack of reliableness of woman's mind."[1]

A further danger to character, arising from the seclusion of woman and the too great emphasis upon her purely physical functions, is that a subtle atmosphhere of animality is thereby introduced into family life. Mere fecundity is too much worshipped in India. It is made a religion. The sacred bull and the phallic emblem of Śiva, the liṅgaṁ, are the universal symbols of this worship. It is a fashion nowadays to regard as unwholesome sentimentality any effort to suppress what is purely natural. Some of the psycho-analysis theories would refer many forms of neuroses to such checks. According to these theories one would expect to find, in a land where sex has been deified and where nature is in many respects untrammelled and unpruned, a nervous balance and serenity to prove the contention of the new theorists. But it is not so. Many Bengali women are noticeably hysterical and neurotic, whatever the cause.

Humanity in its noblest development has struggled to elevate the relation of the sexes and to make of parenthood the finest responsibility that man and woman can take upon themselves. It is possible that in some sections of Christian society we have been tempted in this matter to "wind ourselves too high for sinful man beneath the sky," but it has been an error in the right direction. Restraint and reticence bear fruits that cannot be dispensed with in the highest civilisation. It is not mere puritan prejudice that makes one see, in the precocious parentage of a youth of sixteen and a girl of twelve, something too purely physical, something so common and perfunctory that it robs the

[1] *Manu*, viii. 77.

marriage relationship of its ideal character and love of its eternal mystery. In the overcrowded, overheated air of the zenana, romance is stifled and one feels that elements are absent which are vital to the loftiest view of family life.

It is not that the Hindu has not a high standard of chastity for woman, for it is held that by being chaste a woman is protected as by a magic circle from evil, and wields a peculiar power in the presence of danger. A common saying is: "By chastity the poorest woman becomes a queen." It may be a somewhat narrow standard of the "thou shalt not" order, but it has permeated all classes of society. The standard, as in so many human societies, is apt to be a double one, but a higher ideal exists in the words from the Hindu scriptures: "Let there be mutual fidelity ending in death alone; this in few words should be recognized as the highest law of duty for man and wife. . . . Thus has been declared to you this rule of right in regard to man and wife (a rule) founded on love."

Notwithstanding this ideal and the blameless character of the majority of Hindu married women, there exists among Indians generally a cynical unbelief in the power of woman to guard her own purity. She must have external guards and recognized guardians, and for this reason, among others, she must be married very young. She is given no chance to develop self-control in this respect, and if she is frail when exposed to danger, it is the system and not herself that must be blamed. Yet the wisdom of Manu saw the evil of such a view of woman's weakness and he wrote: "Women are not guarded by being confined at home."[1]

But even Manu was not proof against the prevailing doubt, for in the same code one finds such a passage as this

[1] *Manu*, ix. 12.

(and one has heard it quoted as authoritative at the present day): "One should not be seated in a secluded place with a mother, sister and daughter. The powerful host of the senses compels even a wise man."[1] Only in a society where men and women are habitually segregated could so morbid a fear of innocent companionship have arisen. One would fain think that such a view belonged to an ancient, uncultivated and unstable state of society; but these words were heard recently: "You Englishwomen are not like us. Your senses are cold. For us even a brother's glance means embarrassment." It may be possible to trace this exaggeration of self-consciousness to climatic conditions, lack of healthful exercise, and other unavoidable causes. But surely it is, at least in part, due to causes that might be removed. A later marriage age would ensure the comradeship of sisters and brothers in early youth, and would accustom fathers to the intimate and affectionate relationship, free from emotionalism, that is possible between a parent and his daughter even in young womanhood. A purer religion would cast out the phallic element, which tinctures so much of popular myth and worship and gives sanction to that precocious cultivation of sex instinct and insistence upon the glories of fecundity which colour too strongly the domestic and social laws of Bengal.

It is difficult to find any justification for the splitting up of society into two classes with a great gulf between, or to discover in what respect India has reaped any benefit from it. The risks of freedom are great, no doubt, but they are as nothing compared with the risks of bondage. The following cutting from a Hindu magagine reveals an attitude all too common. (The name of magazine and writer have

[1] *Manu*, ii. 215.

not been kept.) "We do not trust our women; we have inherited woman-hatred from our forefathers, and we breathe it in every day in our homes. It has entered our very constitution, and only liberal education can eradicate this deep-seated prejudice in our nature." The pardā system is based primarily on this accepted view of woman, whatever other causes may have contributed to the custom.

It is a relief to turn from such views of woman to the lofty ideal of filial reverence for the mother expressed and exemplified all over India. "By devotion to his mother he obtains the world," says Manu[1] of the good son, and, in spite of woman's depressed condition, there are not absent elements of grace and beauty in the general thought about her. "Let women's names be . . . like words of benediction," says the sacred text,[2] and the words symbolise a universal belief in woman's power to bless. The injunction to choose sweet-sounding words has been obeyed, and the poetry of common life finds expression in the names of Hindu girls; stars and flowers, words denoting qualities of beauty and virtue, and the names of beneficent goddesses, are the common sources from which they are derived. An Indian speaks of his mother with reverence that one recognises as real.

Since this is undoubtedly one of those things in which India has risen to a height worthy of herself, it is a fitting note on which to end this chapter. "A teacher surpasses in venerableness ten sub-teachers; a father a hundred teachers; but a mother a thousand fathers." This ancient text is still the motto of the good Hindu and the safeguard of woman's place in Indian society. Its worth and sincerity are the foundation upon which a future of better things for her will surely be built.

[1] *Manu*, ii. 233. [2] *Manu*, ii. 33.

CHAPTER V

THE WOMAN'S WORLD

For the Bengali woman life is divided into two main sections: the period spent in her *bāper bārī* or father's house, and that spent in her *śaśur bārī* or father-in-law's house. The first period is brief compared with the second, unless, as sometimes happens, she returns to her father's house as a widow and spends the remainder of her life there. But the early years, though few, often leave a strong mark on a girl's life, and she carries with her into her married state ideas and prepossessions which make her relation to her new home either conflict or harmonise with her former one. The ancient practice of marrying girls in their childhood, and even babyhood, made this change in past times less abrupt, and in some ways less of an ordeal than at the present day. It has always been one of the arguments in favour of very early marriages that the change of environment was made before the girl had become too strongly attached to her parents and household, and at an age when she could enter light-heartedly into the new home, where sweets and pretty clothes and cossetting reconciled her to the strange "mother." Bengali marriage nowadays is neither one thing nor another; neither child-marriage nor adult-marriage; but means in many cases the sudden introduction of a self-conscious and trembling girl of thirteen or fourteen to an unknown husband and to all the stern realities of wifehood and maternity—with results that are sometimes a tragedy.

For the great majority of women, education, in the sense of "schooling," ends at the time of marriage—that is about eleven or twelve years—so that even when women are described in a census as literate, it seldom means more than an ability to read and write a childish letter. The few years spent at a primary school or in playing at lessons with her brothers' tutor or pandit, make but a faint and sometimes fleeting impression upon her intelligence.

There is a section of Bengali society that has begun to take the education of girls seriously, but what has been said is still true of the majority of orthodox and middle-class households, and of course applies almost without exception to the poorer classes. Wealth, unless accompanied by modern ideas of education, does not of itself necessarily make any difference. In fact, the wealthiest classes are not the most progressive in this respect. In some of the great family mansions of Calcutta one finds a childish state of illiteracy and ignorance among the women. In these old-fashioned establishments the women are in a less enviable position than their poorer sisters; for the latter have household tasks to quicken their faculties, whereas the latter are waited on by troops of servants and spend a great part of their time in sheer idleness.

A Hindu gentleman, speaking of the enforced idleness of women so situated, declared that it made them light, frivolous, and even immoral. But his judgment may have been too severe. It is not easy for an outsider to form an opinion on the matter, even although isolated cases show that unhappy intrigue is not rendered impossible by strict seclusion. Even when these women are permitted to drive out, the carriage or motor car is shut up so that they see very little of the outside world, and thus even this natural source of knowledge is denied them. The last few years have witnessed somewhat rapid changes in this respect, and it is no longer regarded as outrageous for women of good family to drive out in only semi-concealed fashion. Emancipated society does not observe these restrictions at all.

It is difficult to imagine the mental state of persons whose lives are so devoid of healthy activity; and, although one is not prepared to state positively that ennui, discontent, and restlessness are the result of such an existence, yet, from the women of certain classes an outsider gathers the impression of minds that are empty and trivial in youth, flat and complacent in middle-age, and dreary in later life, although at the same time *capable of better things* and only handicapped by unjust social prejudices.

What are the prevailing interests of the pardānaśin? It would not be far from the truth to say that, the moment a girl is born into a Hindu family, the problem of her marriage is born too, and becomes a daily increasing incubus upon the mind of her family, and, as she comes to understand the situation, upon her own young mind also. Recently when a certain Hindu postmaster was shot dead at his post by armed thieves, a public subscription was raised, not primarily to relieve his widow, but to make possible the marriage of his two little daughters. The money would thus benefit the future fathers-in-law rather than the mother of the girls.

The pressure of the necessity of early marriage and the accumulating of a dowry makes itself felt in all that affects the girl's physical and mental condition. In the present day it has acted as a spur to girls' education, since educated families now demand some degree of literacy in the future wives of heir sons. Almost every mother who can find the means, sends her daughter during her childhood to school. As the child reaches the age of eleven or so, and catches the busy eye of the professional matchmaker, it becomes necessary, with a view to getting suitable offers of marriage, to do all that can be done to enhance her physical charms. The young Bengali girl is accustomed from an early age to hear herself appraised as to her future probable value and chances in the marriage market. Better food, careful oiling and treatment of the hair and skin, and training in deportment are applied to develop her natural graces, and various devices are used to camouflage her defects. This chapter in domestic life is racily treated in the story, entitled *The Ugly Bride*, by Sāntā Chatterjee.

Religious training, if such it can be called, is also coloured by this predominating consideration. A girl's earliest religious exercises and prayers are directed to Śiva, and have as their aim the obtaining of a good husband. A little girl of six, when asked by the writer what she intended to do with the fallen blossoms of a creeper which she was seen eagerly gathering in a corner of her sāṛī, replied: "I must make my Śiva pūjā," and one pictured this tiny creature gravely making a mud image of the good-natured god, and laying before it her offering of flowerheads, while she repeated to the dictation of some older woman a rhymed prayer, that she might obtain the boons of a husband like Rāma, a brother-in-law like Lakshman, and herself become a wife like Sītā ; to these innocent petitions there is sometimes added an imprecatory prayer against any possible co-wife who might dispute her claims to the undivided affection of this model husband. Another half-playful rite practised by girls is called "brother pūjā," and is a domestic ceremony not requiring the office of a priest. The sister makes a sign on her brother's forehead while she repeats the words: "My brother is my golden *bhāṭā*" (a very hard fruit, symbolizing a robust and hardy constitution), "let thorns fall upon the door of Yama" (the god of death), i.e., let the door be blocked against his entrance. Thorn fences are used in the country to keep out wild beasts, and one of the practical jokes practised at weddings by the boys of the family is to guard the door of the bridal room against the bridegroom with thorny branches in their hands, and refuse him admission until he pays toll to get in. The brother feast is observed in later life also, and is a celebration of kindly family feeling.

During the period of childhood a Hindu girl has perfect freedom, and shares the open-air life and pleasures of her brothers, if she has any. In a large family house there is usually a great number of boys and girls. At this stage a girl is often treated with indifference, and sometimes contempt. What is a girl, after all, but a drain upon the family resources, one who subtracts from, but never adds anything to, the family fortunes? A young Bengali mother, with an infant daughter at her breast, said to the writer: "When a girl child is born, she should be throttled at once." But her actions belied her jesting words, for, even as she uttered them, she laughed and kissed the face of her baby. A sign of the different estimates of a girl's and boy's birth is the fact that a woman is counted ceremonially unclean for only twenty-one days after the birth of a boy, but thirty days after that of a girl.

Among certain sects virgin-worship is practised in preparation for Kālī-worship. Young girls of the Brāhman caste are taken for the time being as representatives of Kālī, *Śaktir aṁśa*, symbols of the divine energy. This worship is sometimes conducted privately, but more often at Kālī temples, where girls of the *purohit*, or priest caste, are made the objects of certain rites. These rites are not necessarily orgiastic, but many Hindus regard them as leading to abuses, especially when, as sometimes happens, libations of country liquor are used, and the worshippers (and even the young virgin) become intoxicated. Worship of a married woman whose husband is living, *sadhavā* pūjā, is of the same nature, and is observed on the eighth lunar day of the Durgā festival. Every woman should be regarded as part of *śakti*, the divine female energy. This worship has the same merit as Durgā-worship. It is difficult to reconcile this temporary deification of woman with her low spiritual status, but it is just another of those contradictions of which Hinduism is full. In *Mālinī*, a play of Dr. Tagore's, this readiness of Hindu popular worship to deify woman is vividly presented.

It is extremely difficult for any European to gain first-hand knowledge of these practices or to get the better class of educated Hindu to admit that these forms of worship in their more sinister manifestations are still common in Bengal. Many Hindus are themselves ignorant on the subject of popular religious practices, and the women are still more ignorant. One orthodox Hindu admitted to the writer that an intoxicated woman devotee had asked for the use of his little daughter for the celebration of "girl pūjā." He refused her request, as he explained, "Because of the tipsy condition of the wretched woman."[1]

To the average young girl such religious practices are mere hearsay. It is in the preparation and feasts associated

[1] It is quite usual among respectable Hindu women to observe the custom of girl- or wife-worship in an informal, innocent, and almost playful way.

with the greater festivals of the Hindu religious year that she is a gleeful participant. To her they appear more as occasions of jollity than of religious awe. Even if her own home be too poor for a separate celebration, there is sure to be some great house in her lane or pārā in which an imposing new image of clay is set up in the family shrine and duly adorned, consecrated and worshipped in the open court, where she may slip in with the crowd of relatives and guests and watch the pageant in all its thrilling stages. She sees the strange visage of the idol appear in clouds of incense, and listens to the chanted mantras (religious incantations) and the loud clanging of bells and gongs. In this worship she, like other girls of her own age, has no part save that of an onlooker, but familiarity with the picturesque ritual helps to form the background of her religious consciousness and supplies the figures and symbols round which her religious imagination will in the future play; for with its powerful sensuous appeal such ceremonial makes an impression on the child memory far more intense than more austere and spiritual forms of worship. Similar scenes may be witnessed daily at the Hindu temples dotted over the city. On greater occasions, the girl may be taken to one of the more celebrated shrines, such as Kālighāt or Dakshiṇeśwar, but the coming of the image into the family court is attended with more excitement for the children than the more public worship of the common shrines.

Another frequent and delightful source of entertainment is a wedding. Certain seasons being regarded as specially auspicious for marriages, every evening at such times sees the streets thronged with wedding processions. They are of a kind to rejoice a child's heart, and reflect also a certain childlikeness in the mind of adult Orientals.

The splendour of the pageant is in proportion to the wealth of the families concerned. At the present day much of the pageantry is mere mimicry of past glories, a representation in paper and bamboo of the real parts of the processions of bygone days. Instead of the actual elephants, camels, liveried retinue, and chariot-loads of dancing girls, which composed the bridal train, the wedding procession caterers nowadays furnish grotesque imitations of animals and human beings, which are dragged along on wheels. Life-sized puppets, jerked about with strings, take the place of the dancing girls, and the troops of servants carrying torches, a necessity for any company travelling in olden times through the country by night, are represented by coolies bearing acetylene lamps. One imagines that the unpleasant fumes of this gas must be inseparably linked in the minds of many a bride and bridegroom with the great event of their youth.

A "wedding house," as the scene of the ceremony is called (marriages are performed by the family priest in the bride's home), is open to the public, and the little Hindu girl is an eager spectator of the glories attendant on one of her own age and perhaps an intimate playmate. She not unnaturally looks forward to the day when she may occupy the central place in a similar scene of splendour. She recks not of the other side of the picture: the harassing anxieties of the parents who have to find the wherewithal to pay for all this display,[1] and to organise the feasts and hospitalities to a great crowd of wanted and unwanted

[1] "The social life even of the poorest workers is characterised by what, from the economic point of view, can only be described as recklessness. . . . Probably in no country in the world where the average production is so low, do the inhabitants expend so large a proportion of their resources upon social obligations." *India in 1924-25*, L. F. Rushbrook Williams.

guests; the ever-present dread of failing in some expected courtesy, or wounding the highly susceptible *amour propre* of the bridegroom's family; and the chagrin of finding very often, in spite of all their efforts, dissatisfaction, contempt and sometimes bitter wrath on the part of the wedding guests—emotions given expression to in no uncertain voice.[1] The girl's turn may come soon enough for all these worries and humiliations; but to her childish fancy it is all pleasure and glory and splendid fun.

As to the more serious side of a girl's early life, discipline has more to do with deportment than with character. Beyond an injunction to make *praṇāma* (bow the head when passing a shrine) she does not receive any systematic religious training. Dharma, or piety, for her will consist in submission to her husband and his family.[2] Her relations during her childhood to her own family are easy-going, and not supposed to have any great significance in her after-life. She is seldom petted or taken much notice of. Some petting may fall to her share as a young wife if she takes the fancy of her mother-in-law, or if, as sometimes happens, in spite of the highly conventional nature of marriage, her youthful husband falls in love with his girl wife. Such happiness, however, must be surreptitious and unconfessed. It is not considered fitting for a young man to lose his head over his wife. The following is a quotation from the letter of a learned Hindu gentleman on this subject: "The Brāhmanic revival[3] not only required a Hindu woman to regard her husband with sentiments verging on worship, but also to perform definite duties to the members of his family. 'Be like Sītā,' means that a woman should not only be true to her husband and share his joys and sorrows,

[1] *Vide supra*, p. 59. [2] *Vide supra*, p. 63.

[3] A period covering the last six centuries.

but that she should serve her father-in-law, mother-in-law, and the rest of the members of her husband's family, including the servants, with love, affection and kindness. . . . The Brāhmans, however, do not enjoin the same degree of love and attention on the husband in regard to the wife; nay, if a husband loves his wife overmuch, to the neglect of his duties to the other members of the family, he is blamed. . . . No scope is left for romance. . . . Romantic feelings they condemned as disturbing discipline and the equilibrium of the social order."

A young Hindu, recently married, suggested that his wife might visit me accompanied by her mother-in-law—a great concession. When it was proposed that he himself might bring her, he said: "It would not be proper for me to drive out alone with my wife." He was about twenty-five and the girl about fourteen. To many a little wife her husband is almost a stranger, and she regards him with awe if not with actual dread. Comradeship does not thrive readily in an atmosphere so laden with inhibitions, and does not, as a rule, occupy much of a woman's time. Attention to his creature comforts is her first duty, but for companionship he goes to the men's quarters, she to the women's. This, of course, is true of all society to some extent, but much more so in India. As a Bengali husband and father put it to me, "To the husband the wife is a nonentity."

The writer once suggested to a young married lady who was learning English that she might practise certain little phrases in conversation with her husband, who spoke English fluently. "Oh, but I never converse with my husband in that way," she replied with embarrassment. "I do things silently for him and only answer him when he speaks to me." She was the mother of three children. In the home one sees examples of this shyness. Once, in the case of a sixteen-year-old wife, and on another occasion, on a visit to a woman of forty or so, the writer was struck by the nervousnesss displayed when the husband entered the room: fluttering eyelids, trembling lips, and a general exhibition of self-consciousness and emotion showed a lack of the ease of manner one might expect between husband and wife. It made a third person feel like an intruder. Young married couples are not supposed to meet and converse during the day, and must not address each other in the presence of elders. "She behaves just like a memsahib," is said scathingly of a young woman who forgets these proprieties. I fear the English married woman has a reputation in the zenana for shameless "spooning" with her husband. A zealous Bengali friend once defended the writer from such charges by saying that, although she sometimes sat in her husband's room, she always did so at a table with her back turned to him, and occupied with some task. "I know, for I have seen them," she announced triumphantly. It seemed better for one's own reputation and for the sake of one's fellow-countrywomen not to deny the observance of such frigid propriety! But human nature laughs at primness, and one hopes and believes that the sweetness of love's young dream is not denied even to the carefully guarded Bengali wife.

Extraordinary jealousy sometimes exists between a mother and her son's wife, a jealousy not absent from human relations anywhere, but finding in the peculiar social arrangements of the Hindu world an opportunity (which it does not so readily find elsewhere) to display itself, sometimes in very malignant forms. The relation of mother and son in Hindu society is made more intense because his marriage does not separate him from his home. The common English saying, "My son's my son till he gets him a wife, my daughter's my daughter all my life," might almost be reversed in India, for it is the daughter who becomes like another woman's daughter almost in childhood, when her marriage takes place, whereas the son remains at home and submits to his mother in all domestic matters, not excepting the choice of a wife. Even in the matter of cooking for her husband a young wife has to leave the management to her mother-in-law, playing very often no more than the part of a kitchenmaid in the operation.

A mother dreads above all things the estrangement under the family roof of a son too much under the influence of his wife, and sets herself by every means to prevent the loss of her hold over him. Rev. Lal Behari Dey makes one of his characters speak thus in *Bengal Village Life*: "Shall I prefer my wife to my mother? Oh, wicked thought! A man may forsake his wife without sin; but for a man to forsake his mother is the greatest of all sins." On the other hand, a Hindu mother takes great pride in her "bow," or daughter-in-law; and to be able to point to a modest, docile and good-looking girl, and say, "My bow," gives her peculiar satisfaction and pleasure, especially if she has chosen the girl herself and been justified in her choice.

The chief source of happiness in the Hindu woman's world, as has been indicated, lies in motherhood. In this sphere alone is she permitted to live her own life and follow her own natural bent; and whatever hardships may accompany the bearing of the burden of maternity in extreme youth, it still opens for her a realm of innocent joys and pure disinterested spending of herself. One sees many a lovely picture of tender motherhood in the cloistered seclusion of the Bengali home. The desire for children is universal, as is also the love of them, in India. Once, in a

MOTHER AND CHILD.

From the painting by J. Seal.

particularly sordid Calcutta lane, where the signs of wretchedness and degradation were painfully evident, the writer's eye was caught by a great white mass of cotton wool freshly gathered from the pod, and looking like a fall of snow. Beside it stood a poor woman holding above her at arm's length a naked infant. Her eyes were full of ecstatic mother-love and as she gathered the child to her and kissed him again and again the snow-like mass in its dark surroundings became a symbol of the purity of motherhood, which everywhere redeems and sweetens the narrow and often shadowed life of India's women.

Love of her son is the ruling passion of the Bengali woman, at least so it would appear to the onlooker. One cannot probe the secrets of other hearts, but, as far as one can judge from observation, the love of husband, although raised to the level of a religious cult, has not that spontaneous quality of sheer devotion manifest in the relation of mother to son. It is, perhaps, the intensity of this relation that has influenced Hindu religious thought and expression so profoundly. To the Hindu it is the mother aspect of God that calls for his most fervent worship. Says a modern Hindu commentator: "To call the great spirit mother is sweeter, more soul-stirring than anything else."[1] This religious conception reacts upon the common way of life, giving to the name and idea of "mother" a special sweetness and holiness. To conform to the ideal of inexhaustible affection, care and service of the beloved child, summed up in the word, is the ambition of every good Hindu woman.

Just as the worship of the Virgin brought to Europe a new conception of the sacredness of maidenhood and the homage due to it as expressed in chivalry, so in India a woman

[1] B. N. Pal, in *Śiva and Śakti.*

addressed as "mother" knows that she is thereby entitled to consideration and respect. Even little girls are addressed as "Mā," and a man need never be at a loss for a respectful form of address to any woman of whatever rank, age or relation to himself, since "Mā" is appropriate to all.

The mother's love does not, however, exclude her daughters. From time to time her girls return to the paternal roof, rejoicing in the escape from the stricter rule of their mothers-in-law. The mother during these brief holidays gives herself up to an unusually intimate and comrade-like relation with them. There is unrestricted talk and freedom from conventions. The veil is tossed back from the head, and the daughter is a child once more. One can tell that a married girl is in her father's house if the face is unveiled. The mother, eager to retain first place in her daughter's affection, does not altogether frown upon complaints of autocratic and suspicious mothers-in-law, and does not regard comparisons in her own favour as in any way odious. On her daughter's children, born usually under her own care, the mother lavishes a devotion which is a revival of her own early motherhood.

Leaving out of consideration for the moment the religious side of woman's life, which will be referred to in a later chapter, it must be confessed that, apart from her family relationships, the average pardā woman in Bengal has few interests, or none at all, save food, clothing and ornaments. The manner of her life shuts her in to these mundane concerns and gives to them an exaggerated importance; and while it is true that woman will almost have ceased to be woman when these topics of daily occurrence and never-ending import no longer interest her, in Western countries she has at least discovered that other important things are possible of attainment even without the neglect of her chief functions and duties. The majority of zenana women are still quite content to discuss trivial matters continually, and, being deprived of male society, which discourages to some extent exclusively feminine topics, they are shut in to mere "women's talk."

Thoughts about food occupy a great place in the Bengali mind. But it is the quality, and method of preparation rather than the amount of variety of their viands, or the pleasure of eating good things, that concern them. As a race they are quite frankly connoisseurs in delicate eating. They talk of certain famous curries and concoctions with glistening eyes. But the West, too, celebrates wine and even roast beef in song, so we cannot say "gourmand" to anyone. Pleasure in good food is a natural human trait. It may be that the lengthy periods between meals in the East stimulate the longing for and enjoyment of food, while, on the other hand, appetite often fails in the heat and has to be tempted by cunning odours and spices; so that cooking has become a real art and one practised by men and women of all ranks and classes. Caste restrictions make it necessary for a man to be able to cook his own food in certain circumstances, and to contrive all the devices for cooking it well in camp or on a journey. The *al fresco* meal is everywhere common in India, where long journeys on foot through uninhabited regions have to be made.

The tastelessness of the staple food—rice and lentils, cooked, as a rule, without salt—makes a savouriness in its accompaniments necessary. The spices used to make curries are freshly pounded from the seeds every day, so that their full flavour may be enjoyed. Turmeric, ginger, peppers, cardamums, mustard, coriander and cummin seed, etc., blend in a flavour almost overpowering to the European palate, and, when mingled in boiling oil or butter, send up pungent odours that fill the air at morning and evening, when meals are being cooked. This all-pervading odour, with its subtle play on the olfactory nerves, makes the mouth water in a way that the mere roasting of meat or frying of bacon could never do. The wholesome smell of unleavened bread, baked on redhot cinders, has a homeliness that appeals to all appetites. Perhaps the steam of boiling rice is a little too suggestive of washing day to be quite agreeable to Western nostrils, but, no doubt, it bathes the Indian fancy in anticipation of the evening meal at the close of the day's toil.

Unlike other Hindus, Bengalis include fish in their diet.[1] Bengal, with its network of waterways, has an abundant supply of fish, but the better kinds are a luxury and are not usually included in the diet of the poor. Shrimps and prawns are the breakfast "bacon" of the Bengali, and often, by midday, lanes in Calcutta are noisome with the smell of the shells of these crustaceans lying in the rubbish heaps, which even better-class people think no shame to have at their doors.

The average household has two main meals a day, breakfast and supper. Indian women sometimes ask me if it is the case that we have five meals—and by this they mean square meals. This fact they have been told, with much more of a fabulous kind, about the English. The mistake has arisen because our lighter repasts are almost as ceremonious, at least in India, as our chief meals. The Indian who can afford it, has morning and afternoon "snacks" of

[1] Except widows, who are strictly vegetarian.

a fairly substantial kind, corresponding to our morning tea and luncheon or afternoon tea.

No Indian lady thinks it beneath her dignity to cook. It is regarded as an art, and the Hindu housewife prides herself upon her skill. Even when expert Brāhman cooks are kept, the ladies like to help in the preparation of the food, and make certain cakes, sweets and confections of fruit, which are the delicacies of the Indian "table."

Rice is prized and even worshipped in Bengal as a form of Lakshmī, the goddess of good fortune and prosperity. Round it, more than any other necessity of life, except water, gather all the caste restrictions regarding food. It also forms part of the most sacred ceremonies, the offerings to the gods and to the ancestors, the chief element in the śrāddha, or obsequies, being the ball of rice offered by the son. In its passage from field to granary, and from granary to the domestic table or the household and temple shrines, it is hedged about with sacred associations. First fruits for the god, first rice for the weaned son, virgin rice for the betrothed maiden, bride rice for the new daughter-in-law, and the *piṇḍa*, or rice ball, for the dead, are the familiar symbols in which family joys and pieties are expressed, and make part of the natural poetry of human life and society among the Bengali Hindus. In itself rice is beautiful, whether standing thick and green in the rain-flooded fields, or bending its golden heads to the sickle, falling in a pearly shower from the winnowing basket, or, last of all, in a white foam on the glistening brass platter or plantain leaf—the plate of the poor—ready to be eaten. The Bengali thinks of his rice in separate grains, and counts it in handfuls. "Four rices" is the description of a poor meal made by one who has no appetite. Rice is precious because everything in this country depends on the rice crop. "When Mother Lakshmī fails, all fails," is a homely saying. In a verse of the sacred books we find the right regard for food defined : "Let him [the Brāhman] ever reverence food, and let him eat without finding fault with it; having seen it let him rejoice and be satisfied, and let him always receive it gladly. For food that has been reverenced ever bestows strength and power." Another common saying is: "Lo, Anna [food] thou art adored." The sentiments here implied reflect sound psychology and good dietetics. It has been observed that Bengalis "give much thought to the mental effect of what is eaten."

To a peace-loving race like the Hindus of Bengal there is satisfaction, no doubt, in partaking of food that necessitates no hunting or slaughter of animals or even risk to human life. The ingredients of the daily meals grow about their doors in garden, orchard and field in abundance at every season. Famine is rare in Bengal, although floods sometimes destroy the crops. It is difficult to recruit labour for industries in Bengal, because there are food and work for the great bulk of the population, thanks to the teeming harvests. True, the very poor have to be content with the barest necessities, and subsist on rice with a pinch of salt, or parched rice without even the salt. The common accompaniments of rice are *dāl* (lentils), mustard oil, and vegetables of the pumpkin or tuber varieties. A kind of large plantain is plentiful and very nourishing. Cabbage, cauliflower and potatoes, of more recent introduction than the others, are prime favourites.

The most nourishing and luxurious element in Bengali diet is ghee, or clarified butter. It is really a necessity because of the lack of fat in the food, but, owing to the high price of milk and all milk products in recent times, many of the people go without it, substituting vegetable oils. The want of ghee is a serious menace to the stamina of the race, and children especially are noticeably under-nourished in many homes. A common saying, "Ghee must be got, even if it entails borrowing money to buy it," shows that the people are alive to its food value.

All the products of milk, especially the sweets made from compressed fresh curd and various syrups, are coveted by rich and poor alike as the most nourishing and delicious food available. But the poor can eat but sparingly of them; for their price is high, and has greatly increased of late years. Butter is eaten by itself, very fresh and mixed with sugar candy. It is also mixed with boiled rice, and occasionally spread on unleavened bread. The milk of the cow is scant and poor in quality, owing to the lack of green pasture, so it requires a great quantity to produce a small amount of butter. Buffalo milk, which is rich in butter, is not liked by Bengalis, as it is considered heating. Children and invalids are often fed with goats' milk.

Bengalis are notoriously fastidious about their food. Many factors have contributed to this sensitiveness, the chief being caste prejudice, and capricious appetite owing to heat and fevers. Apart from caste precautions, eating is a much simpler affair with them than with us. It is one of the rules regarding rice that it must be placed on the ground. Other articles of food may be eaten standing, but rice can only be eaten by the orthodox sitting on the floor. So this mode of taking meals is not considered undignified by the highest in the land. Each person has his own platter, of slate or bell metal. Sometimes, if the meal is an elaborate one, the platter is as large as a tray, and has smaller plates and bowls set on it. Everything is eaten with the fingers, even to the all-but-liquid sour curd, which is taken along with the sweet course. This may seem to unaccustomed eyes unfastidious, but probably Europe would still be eating with its fingers, if it were not for the great discomfort of dipping the fingers into food as hot as it is usually consumed. We still eat with our fingers bread, fruit, and other things that can easily be so eaten. In eating rice the first three fingers are used as a spoon, and the food is pushed neatly into the mouth with the thumb. The fingers are not put into the mouth. Meals are not as a rule social, as with us. Eating separates rather than unites. It is usual for different members of the household to eat alone. The wife does not eat with her husband, but attends him while he eats. She does the same for her family, herself eating after all have been fed, even the servants. This is, at all events, the ideal for the good housewife. A strict Hindu does not talk while eating. At feasts the social part, talking, music, nautch or play, takes place before the meal, which is silent.

As a matter of curiosity the writer once asked an orthodox Brāhman if, apart from mental conviction as to its undesirability, he would experience actual repugnance in partaking of food touched by anyone not of the proper caste. "Oh, yes, yes!" he exclaimed with a shudder; and it was easy to see that his feeling was genuine. By way of illustration he related how, in his wife's home the womenfolk had for some time eaten rice cooked by a Brāhman widow. When they discovered that this woman was not of good character and had associated with Muhammadans, they were so distressed that they were seized with violent sickness, and for many days were unable to swallow rice. The tale was told so simply that one could not doubt its truth and it is easy enough to imagine how such sensitiveness might develop when eating is so hedged about with restrictions.

Nature is lavish in Bengal, and at every season of the

year fruits are to be obtained. Some of the trees are highly valued, because they yield not only fruit but many other household articles, especially the cocoanut, whose leaves, fibres and shells, as well as the fruit and oil, are in daily use. The oil is applied to hair and skin, the fibre made into rope, matting and stuffing for mattresses, the veins of the long leaves are tied in bunches to make brooms; the empty shell is used as a bowl for the hookah, the half shell as a natural cup for kitchen use, and fruit and "milk" as food and beverage. The tree, which is sacred, is spoken of fondly, and called a "Brāhman" among trees because of its many virtues.

Other common trees highly valued are the mango, whose luscious fruit is considered by some people the finest in the world; the jack tree, whose fruit, similar to, but coarser than, the bread fruit, sometimes weighing forty pounds, provides a feast for a company (the skin and seed make good food for cattle; so that nothing is wasted); the bael, much prized for its medicinal properties, and the lichu, custard-apple, and other trees, cultivated all over Bengal, whose fruit is delicious and beneficial. Indians long ago discovered the value of fruit as food, especially in connection with illnesses of various kinds, and knew practically, if not theoretically, where vitamins existed in most abundance. Plantains provide two kinds of fruit—the sweet plantain, which is eaten raw, and the green plantain (*kānchkalā*), which is cooked, and has remarkable nourishing and sustaining qualities. It is little used by Europeans, because of its tastelessness and unattractive appearance when cooked, but Bengalis use it for invalids and puny children, and eat it before a fast to fortify themselves.

The areca-nut palm yields the astringent nut, which is chopped in tiny morsels, and, along with betel (an aromatic leaf) chewed daily after food. The chopping of the nut is one of the daily tasks of the Indian woman, and there is scarcely a commoner sight in the home than the nut-cracker at work. It is hard work, and requires dexterity to shred the hard fibre—like a nutmeg's—but it is done in odd moments almost as a pastime. The pieces of nut are wrapped in the leaf, on which quicklime has been spread, some spices and catechu are added, and the little packet rolled up and secured by a clove used as a pin. When chewed, the combination of leaf juice and lime forms a brilliant red colour, which stains the mouth. This bright red on the lips of girls is greatly admired. A story is told of an Indian gentleman at an official reception who, admiring the too carmine lips of a young English lady to whom he had been introduced, said he was much gratified, if he might take the liberty of saying so, to observe that she had adopted the Indian habit of taking betel! Too much pān chewing has a deleterious effect on the teeth and causes them to turn black, but this may be due to the addition of narcotics, which habitual pān chewers indulge in. Curious formalities have grown up round the offering and receiving of pān supāri, not unlike wine ceremonies in Europe, or tea ceremonies in China. Honoured guests are offered pān in a silver dish, and official guests are expected to receive it even if they do not eat it. Indians are greatly pleased if a foreigner both accepts and eats it, and laugh delightedly when the familiar stain appears on his lips. A dancing girl, performing before company, is dismissed by handing her a pān supāri. The reason for pān chewing is supposed to be that it exercises the teeth and causes a flow of saliva after meals, an effect not sufficiently produced by the pulpy diet of rice and vegetables.

Dress does not receive much attention from the Bengali

woman after she has passed her earliest years of married life; nor is vanity about her personal appearance one of her failings; yet she has a true instinct for dress and has inherited from antiquity a robe, and manner of wearing it, that is perfectly suited to her surroundings, being simple, economical and beautiful. The sāṛī is a long piece of muslin or silk (about six and a half yards), with a woven edge of black or colour. It is wide enough to reach from waist to ankle. Muslin is the everyday material of Bengal. For special occasions a richer material is worn. For the orthodox Bengali woman of every class the simple sāṛī, skilfully wound and drapped about the figure to form a double petticoat, shawl and veil, is a complete and dignified dress. She wears nothing else, summer and winter, except when she goes out. In the case of young wives, however, it is often a sign of petting when they are given a pretty jacket or other extra garment to wear. Among emancipated women, school girls and students, a more elaborate costume has been adopted, their more public life making this a necessity. The sāṛī by itself is sometimes an insufficient protection from cold, and there can be no doubt that the prevalence of dysentery, cholera, and kindred ailments, is due in part to the chills that are inevitable when a woman passes from the cookroom into draughty verandah or courtyard. It is possible also that the increasing susceptibility of the women of Calcutta to tuberculosis may be due to the insufficiency of their clothing. The great variations of temperature in the hot weather, and the lowered resistance to the effects of such changes following upon fevers, constitute an always present danger to health, especially when to these are added a diet not always sufficiently nourishing even in good homes, irregularity of meals, and inattention to the simple laws of hygiene. Where these matters receive attention, as in a well-conducted girls' boarding school, it is significant that the general health is very much better than in the zenanas even of wealthy houses.

The sāṛī is a graceful dress, and it is useless to deny that it is chiefly so when it is the sole garment. Worn by a slender and pretty young woman, it imparts a classic beauty to the lines of the figure. When it covers the head and veils the face of the new bride, it lends an air of mystery that is attractive and symbolical of the reverence that ought to attach to marriage and motherhood. These veiled ones are like the novitiates in some religious order, or like the Madonnas of early art. In itself the sāṛī may be a thing of great beauty, and for special occasions the plain cotton garment is laid aside for one of silk or silk muslin, with border and ends of intricately woven designs in spun gold or silver thread. These finer sāṛīs are made on handlooms, and are works of art of which any country might be justly proud. Dacca, Benares and other places are famous for the fineness of their weaving and the dexterity of their craftsmen, whose knowledge has been hereditary from ancient times. The Greeks remarked the delicacy of Indian webs, and in ancient Indian poetry we find references to the beauty of fair women clad in dark blue muslin, like the moon in the night sky.[1] For great occasions nothing but the splendour of silk, so richly interwoven with gold designs as to be almost cloth of gold, is considered fitting. Such dresses are, of course, costly, owing to the fine materials used and the labour involved in producing them. But they are very enduring, and become family heirlooms. When the cloth is worn out, the garment is burnt and the gold extracted, to be woven anew

[1] *Indo-Aryans*, Rajendralal Mitra, vol. i. p. 176: "The art of making the finest webs is all but lost nowadays."

into a fresh garment. Few households are so impoverished as not to possess one or two specimens of fine handweaving. When on a journey, a woman adds a sheet or shawl of heavier cotton, silk, or woollen material, but these are rarely worn in the house.

However simple her garment may be, the most significant part of a woman's dress is her ornaments. Every married woman must wear some gold bracelets. To be without any is the universal mark of widowhood. It is by the quality of her ornaments that one guesses the worldly position of a woman. The entire panoply is worn only on the wedding day and other ceremonial occasions. A woman tends to wear less as she becomes elderly, but she must always wear some gold, especially bracelets, while her husband is alive.

A girl's ornaments are an important part of her dowry, and, if her present and future relatives are wealthy, she is often weighed down by the mass of jewellery considered fitting for her wedding array. Every part of her person is adorned: a chaplet of gold thickly set with gems for the head, medallion-shaped coverings for the ears, or a series of jewelled rings round the entire rim of the ear, which is ruthlessly punctured during her childhood, gold pins and nets for the hair, jewelled drops or rings for the nose, which is pierced at the side or in the cartilege between the nostrils, a jewelled collar for the neck, sundry chains and necklaces of great weight, made of small medallions set with jewels, and strings of pearls, form a breastplate of splendour; gold bands and bangles for the upper arm, bracelets and cuffs of gold for the wrists, rings for the fingers, and a heavy zone of gold for the waist, probably the ancient symbol of virginity—all these are duly donned by a wealthy bride.

Here the gold ornaments end, at least in Bengal. The anklets and toe-rings are silver, and are composed of clusters of tiny bells that make a musical tinkling wherever a girl goes. This tinkling sign of a young girl's approach is often referred to in Indian poetry Among the gold articles worn there will be one hidden in the woman's bosom, a locket containing a precious charm against sickness or barrenness, or the evil eye. A woman wins social recognition at Hindu gatherings by the wealth of her jewels. If she has only a few, she is regarded as a person of little consequence, unless, of course, she is a widow. Widows do not wear ornaments. It is not considered proper in a young hushand to give, or a wife to receive from him, any costly gift in the form of jewellery. Such gifts are made by her father-in-law. Her appearance and dress are supposed to reflect credit upon the latter. She is pointed out in society, not as So-and-so's wife, but as So-and-so's " bow," or daughter-in-law. The orthodox Hindu lady in Bengal does not wear shoes. Her bare and shapely feet, delicately cared for and ornamented on the sole with red lac to enhance their fairness, are her pride. Sculptors would do well to seek their models for an unspoiled human foot among Indian women. The " lotus feet " of women are the subject of poetry, and feet as a symbol find their place in religion. Many religious charms have the footprints of some god stamped on them, and footprints are the markings on memorial stones in some parts of India. The actual footprints of the dying, taken in red colour on cloth or stone, are kept as a sacred relic and object of worship, especially by widows.[1]

The wearing of shoes, now become common because necessary among emancipated Indian women who appear

[1] *Vide infra*, p. 111.

THE SARI.

From the painting by H. Mazumdar.

in public, was, and still is in some circles, regarded as frivolous or even immodest. In older literature and sculpture only women not modest are depicted as wearing shoes—a sign that they did not keep to the home. Dr. Tagore illustrates this sentiment in a passage in *The Home and the World*: "Once, in the old days, when Bimala had not yet overcome her objection to shoes, I had got these out from Lucknow to tempt her. The first time she was ready to drop for very shame to go in them, even from the room to the verandah."[1]

This passage illustrates also incidentally a woman's shrinking from doing anything contrary to custom.

"In *The Little Clay Cart*, of Śūdraka (about the fifth century A.D.), the mother of a rich courtesan is described as arrayed in flowered muslin, with her feet thrust into a pair of slippers, showing that, in ancient times, as in the present day, women of the town were in the habit of wearing shoes. Whether family women ever used them I have not yet been able to discover; but there is no text forbidding such use that I am aware of."[2]

In the great heat of the Indian plains, comfort rather than elegance is the first consideration in dress. The excessive perspiration makes the continual washing (or at least a kind of half-washing, sometimes partly ceremonial) of the sāṛī a necessity. The white sāṛī is apt to look dingy in consequence. There is an underlying idea that, for a woman past her first youth to give much thought to her appearance and dress is coquettish and unwomanly. The young wife has her hair prettily braided and her skin, hands and feet tended by others, but when these attentions cease, it does not usually occur to her to carry on the process

[1] Op. cit., p. 124.

[2] *Indo-Aryans*, Rajendralal Mitra, vol. ii. p. 223.

for herself. In fact, she would probably be teased and laughed at if she did so.

The tendency to low spirits, so marked in Bengali women, seems to be reflected in the everyday dress; and the dullness of a white sāṛī (not really as white as it might be), which, except on gala occasions, is the usual wear, robs woman of one of her natural sources of gaiety. Modern life is altering this. Woman's passion for dress has been suppressed, but by no means obliterated, by the sobrieties of the secluded life, and the Bengali woman does not really enjoy being dowdy any more than her sisters elsewhere. Whether the change to a livelier interest in everyday dress is an advantage or otherwise, let dress moralists decide.

Lady Dufferin, in her charming memoirs, relates how often she was made to feel dowdy by the richness of the dress and ornaments of the Indian ladies who received and visited her. But such times would call forth their greatest efforts. The habitual indoor and outdoor freshness of a fastidious Englishwoman are not matched by the rumpled household sāṛī of even well-to-do Indian women. On public occasions, however, such as pardā functions at great houses, where one sees Indian women of rank and wealth in all the bravery of cloth of gold and costly gems, one has to confess that the daintiness of European dress pales into insipidity. Tinkling and rustling, and carrying a breeze of exotic perfumes of sandalwood and attar of roses, the Indian lady has a gorgeousness not aspired to by the average Western woman. The use of cosmetics is not customary among Bengali women. Young girls sometimes have their eyes outlined with a black powder and their cheeks and lips tinted red. But even this is unusual. The chief indigenous cosmetic is sandalwood paste, which is sometimes laid on the brow and cheeks in a lacelike design, and lends a very quaint appearance not unbecoming to little girls. No grown woman adorns herself in this way.

As in all countries, dress has its symbolism. The end of the sāṛī, twisted scarf-like round the neck, is the sign of reverence in service or worship. The nuptial knot is the actual tying of the cloth worn by bride and bridegroom, to show that thus they are bound for life. The pilgrim wears a cloth stamped all over with the names of the gods, and the ascetic has a coarse garment dyed with saffron. The veil is the universal sign of wifehood, and the white borderless and patternless cloth, of widowhood. Red is the colour of joy, and is always donned by the bride during the chief part of the bridal ceremony. White by itself is for mourning, and is never a joyous symbol.

During the periods of relaxation from household duties, the Bengali woman has little by way of amusement to pass the time. Now that it is not unusual for women of the better classes to be able to read, novel-reading has become very popular, and, in the opinion of some, very mischievous, as a great deal of trash is written in these days of cheap printing. The playing of cards is a favourite diversion, but it is not usual to play for money. Of active recreation, walking, outdoor games, dancing, and so on, there is almost none. Even singing and playing musical instruments were, until recently, forbidden to women of respectable households, as they were customary among loose women, dancing girls and actresses. This prejudice, thanks chiefly to the influence of the Tagore family, who have created a new type of songs, has been removed to some extent; and music, albeit of a very crude kind in most cases, is becoming a favourite pastime among girls and young married women.

Story-telling is still one of the chief recreations, the old ladies of the household being the caterers. The stories have charm for young and old alike; and some of the older women have an unlimited repertory. The songs of wandering minstrels, some of which are beautiful and poetic ballads,[1] the recitations by *Kathakas* of the sacred dramas, an occasional snake-charmer, monkey-man or juggler, listened to or watched under due supervision, break the monotony of seclusion from time to time. Theatre-going has become very popular in recent days, but is not permitted to most of the women except as a very rare privilege. Picture houses are even more popular, and are sometimes crowded with women, notably on *Śivarātrī*, when an all-night vigil has to be kept, and this device for keeping awake has been discovered! Most theatrical performances are Oriental, but the films are largely Western and often extremely vulgar, and a ridiculous travesty of European and American life. From them, it is to be feared, many uneducated Indian women are gathering their ideas of the life of woman when she is free.

Religious pilgrimages might almost be included under the head of the recreational element in a Bengali woman's life. When a woman reaches an age at which she can lay aside the duties of the home and go on a visit to some sacred city or shrine, she looks forward to it with an excitement not altogether religious, and as a rule enjoys every part of the experience and comes back full of her adventures and with tales to last for conversation for many a day. More usually it is the widows who undertake these journeys. Although they face a certain amount of hardship, it is the sort of hardship we associate with a picnic—a kind of exhilarating venturesomeness. The writer recently

[1] Cf. the writings of Dinesh Chandra Sen.

A WOMAN PILGRIM.

From a photograph by Miss R. Hardie.

persuaded a widow to talk about her latest pilgrimage, which was to Baidyanāth and taken in company with friends and servants. One could gather from what she said that it was change of air, scene and companionship, the freedom from the worries and bickerings of family life, and the physical refreshment of life in the open air—she laid great stress on her enormous appetite for her one widow's meal—that were the sources of pleasure. It was only after the idea of spiritual renewal had been suggested to her that she seemed to realize that that was what a religious pilgrimage was primarily arranged to provide, whereupon she admitted rather lamely that it was very peaceful, after climbing a steep hill to a shrine, to feel the solitude and quiet of the mountains, and later to sit weary but refreshed, and listen to the sacred books being read.

The *melās*, or fairs, connected with religious festivals are a source of enjoyment to such women as are permitted to attend them, as are also occasional visits to a temple or to the Ganges on holy days to bathe. Women never go out to shop, but itinerant vendors visit the houses daily, and, if chaperoned by elders, the women are allowed to chaffer with cloth and perfume sellers, etc., in the outer court of their houses.

The natural atmosphere of the Bengali woman's world seems unnatural to us, but I sometimes wonder if, like the blind mole in a story of our childhood, they would tell us: It is nothing when you are used to it. As one grows intimate with household after household, one learns of the common joys and sorrows of the various family histories: granny's aches and worries, mother's anxiety over a turbulent son, or her longing to see a little married daughter too seldom permitted to return to her father's house. "They are unwilling to let her come, and if I insist they may tell me to keep her altogether, as they can easily get another wife for their son," she will tell you sadly.

There is often a background of great trouble and even tragedy. One hears of a cruel mother-in-law, never pleased; of jealousy and strife over children and property; sometimes of a husband who is unfaithful and flaunts his unfaithfulness in the eyes of the neighbourhood to the sorrow and humiliation of his wife. Bereavement is common in a land so full of deadly diseases, and few mothers see all their children grow up. The rate of infant mortality in some parts of Calcutta is so high that one in every four children dies in its first year. Sometimes the amount of sadness seems to swamp all else; and, although the troubles enumerated are common human ills to be met with everywhere, the pardānaśin seems so entirely shut in to them when they befall her, she appears so bound in sorrow and misery without mitigation, that it is little wonder that in most books written about her the shadows are very black and fill the picture. If I have tried to avoid that extreme, it is not because I am not fully alive to the pathos of her life, but because the other side also has to be set forth if one is to have a true picture.

CHAPTER VI

THE BENGALI WOMAN'S RELIGION

To write with knowledge of the religion of the orthodox Hindu women of Bengal is a task of very great difficulty; to write with understanding is perhaps almost an impossibility for anyone not a Hindu. Mere lists and descriptions of feasts and fasts and daily rites and ceremonies do not suffice to indicate either their religious temperament or their spiritual status; and, on the other hand, to attempt to come directly at the inward mood of which these practices are the medium of expression, is beset with peculiar difficulties for a foreigner. Information on the subject is very hard to obtain, either from the women themselves, who are often inarticulate as regards their thoughts, or from those who might be supposed to know at first hand—their fathers or husbands or sons. When the inquirer is a Christian, and a Protestant, and Presbyterian to boot, the difficulty is increased. Protestants have had instilled into them from their infancy the stern anti-idolatrous teachings of the Hebrew Scriptures, and the later revolts of reformed Christianity against outward form have taught them to approach image-worship with an intense and involuntary prejudice, if not hatred, and a profound suspicion that it is a deliberate violation of man's truest religious instincts and a wilful sin against light.

To disengage one's mind from the attitude outlined

above is a necessary preliminary to any true insight into the real condition of things, and, although one may end as one began, with an immovable conviction that idolatry stands between man's soul and the deepest knowledge of spiritual reality, one will at least have learned sympathy with the simple worshipper who, among his symbols, is seeking after God if haply he may feel after Him and find Him.

The other day a Hindu lady introduced me to her family shrine, where an image of Nārāyaṇ, or Vishṇu, in the form of a round black stone known as the *śālagrāma*, was set on a small throne, richly attired in finest silk, gold and gems, with wreaths of flowers festooning his seat. Before the image were ranged vessels of silver and copper prepared for worship. The whole room was swept and garnished for the coming of the attendant priest to carry on the evening pūjā (worship). In front of the shrine a little girl sat plucking white scented flowers from the stems and putting the heads into a brass bowl, and as we looked on, a servant entered with a basket of finest sweetmeats. The entire scene, although toylike in its dimensions, was orderly, prepared with loving care and expressive of a childlike zeal to leave nothing undone that the occasion demanded. "The Hindu finds a satisfaction in the forms and minutiæ decreed by tradition, which to the impatient onlooker from the West is hardly intelligible."[1]

"Mother," I asked, "what does this worship mean to you? What part do you take in it, and with what feelings do you respond to the acts of the priest?"

The answer was given simply and sincerely: "I bow with folded hands and experience a feeling of devotion to Nārāyaṇ when the priest repeats the sacred formula."

[1] *Religions of the East*, Alfred S. Geden, D.D., p. 408.

"Then is it to Nārāyaṇ himself, the invisible one, that you feel this devotion, or to this image set here?" asked the visitor.

"I cannot distinguish," she replied, "it is Nārāyaṇ himself we worship; but I love this *mūrti*—the very image itself, familiar to me on its yearly visit to this house since I entered it a bride, about thirty years ago. Yes, I love it like my 'lapchild' [the name given to an infant in arms, the youngest of the family]. When it goes away to the house of our brethren" (it is a family image, which goes the round of a large family in the course of the year), "I feel very sad, and I rejoice when our turn comes again, as if my child had come back to me."

Here was, as far as a mere observer could tell, a genuine emotion of religious joy. It is not easy to determine its spiritual or moral value, but in itself it was a real feeling. And that is what has to be reckoned with: the deep-seated and passionate love of the devout for the actual forms and symbols of his traditional faith and familiar practices. It is easy to dismiss all this as "pitiful superstition," or at best "mere formalism," but giving names to things does not account for their existence. The speaker on this occasion was no rustic ignoramus, but a woman of wealth and birth, who held the kind of position, as head of a large and important household, which develops character and judgment. Yet there was emotional satisfaction, of what is claimed to be a religious kind, in practices that to a maturer religious consciousness would appear mere childishness.

The attitude of this woman is typical. Further illustrations of a similar kind which might be given would only prove that, for the women at least, orthodox Hindu worship is not mere dead formality, but a thing of genuine belief and devotion. A different impression was created on the visitor's mind when the woman's husband, the head of the house, appeared, and remarked jauntily in English as we were leaving the shrine, "Well, been having a look at our idol, have you?" the remark accompanied by a sight grimace of amusement.

Many Hindus are content to have their priests and womenfolk carry on the traditional rites in a spirit of simple belief. They feel that thus the demands of orthodoxy are satisfactorily met, and that they are free to indulge in a cultured scepticism about the whole business, although willing to be present at the actual ceremony. This attitude, if analysed, would often turn out to be more irrational and childish than that of either bigoted priests or illiterate womenfolk. It seems more fundamentally superstitious, in the more sinister sense of the word, to adopt such a pose; for it is as if they said to themselves: The gods may exist, or they may not; the idol may be truly for the moment the dwelling-place of the god, or it may not. If the gods do not exist, and if the image is a mere stone, my intellectual doubt saves my face. If the gods do exist, and if the idol is inhabited by a powerful spirit who had better be propitiated, then my devout practice saves my soul, and my skin, and my social prestige.

The women, sunk deep in ignorance and pathetic, blind belief although they may be, are at least free from such a charge of insincerity and vacillation. And, like the women, the great mass of the people are "joined to their idols" through the simplicity of their unenlightened minds. It is the so-called intelligentsia among the professedly orthodox Hindus whose conduct strikes the onlooker as disingenuous and weakminded. Faith has been ousted, and fear reigns in its stead. As Vaughan says of the Italians of the sixteenth century, faced with the Protestant revival, "Their intellectual position was fatal to sincerity, their social condition equally so to freedom."[1] A Hindu woman remarked to me recently: "We are caught in a mesh of custom from which there is no escape."

In strict Hindu households, the observance, morning and evening, of the ritual homage paid to the household god is a prime duty both for men and women. This form of worship is carried on both in the homes of orthodox caste people and in the public shrines and temples. It consists in offerings of food, flowers, fruit, sacred *durva* grass, sandalwood paste, and other things, accompanied by appropriate mantras (invocations), the sounding of gongs and bells, and the blowing of conches. The evening worship is simpler in form than the morning, the chief observance being the waving of lights in front of the idol, known as *ārati.* Cooked rice is offered to the god only in Brāhman households. In all others sun-dried rice takes its place. The offerings to the household image are not made by the worshippers themselves, but by the family priest, who is a Brāhman. In a Brāhman household the daily worship of Nārāyaṇ or Śiva does not require the office of a priest, but in all other special feasts and pūjās one of the priestly order of Brāhmans is called in. Besides the formal image of the god, the *tulasī*, or basil plant, which is a favourite of Vishṇu, is seen in most houses, and receives almost divine honours. To water it is a religious duty and a means of gaining merit. The women make offerings to it of flowers and rice.

Woman's part in the daily worship is that of an onlooker. In the case of every god, except Śiva and the *ishṭa Devatā*

[1] *Hours with the Mystics*, Book xix. p. 148.

and Shashṭhī, protectress of women, woman is, strictly speaking, not a worshipper at all, but a spectator. She prepares the materials of worship, and during the repetition of the mantra she blows the conch shell and bows her head, but she may not touch the image after it has been consecrated. The conch shell is blown on all great occasions of family or religious ceremonial by the women. It is also sounded loud during an eclipse, to scare the powers of evil supposed to be unloosed in the unnatural darkness. None but Brāhmans may touch the image while it is inhabited by the god, and, among Brāhmans, only men may do so. Brāhman women have no better place in this matter than non-Brāhmans. In fact, except males of the Brāhman caste, no persons whatsoever, man or woman, can really perform the religious ceremonies of morning and evening worship, except, as has been said, in the case of Śiva pūjā and the service of the ishṭa, or "desired," god. The "desired" god is the secret object of worship for fully initiated Hindus. This initiation is the work of the *guru*, or spiritual adviser, of the household and of individual Hindus. Initiation consists in the whispering of the name of a god in the ear of the disciple. The name must never be divulged. Husbands and wives are supposed to have the same god, but must not reveal it even to each other.[1]

Women as well as men are allowed, are indeed enjoined, to "take their mantra," or become devotees of some particular manifestation of God. The secret god must be chosen from among the redeeming gods, Kālī, Jagadhātrī, Annapūrnā, etc. With the name of the god there is imparted to the disciple a special form of invocation or incanta-

[1] There is a popular belief that anyone revealing the name will be struck with leprosy or dumbness.

tion. This is known as a mantra. The god can be "called" only by means of this mantra, and must be so called, at two periods every day, at least a hundred and eight times by the telling of beads. The name[1] must be repeated so quietly "that the person cannot hear herself." The rosary is often held in the bosom under the sāṛī or in a bag, so that prayer shall be unobtrusive. There is no limit to the number of times the name may be repeated in the course of a day, and by some it is said thousands of times. The phalanges of the fingers are sometimes used in this devout counting, red seeds being employed as markers for the hundreds.

The actual words of the mantra, *vīja* (seed) words, as they are called, have no meaning in themselves, but are mere sounds, such as hoong, doong, hling, kling. For a symbol of the god a little brass cup, saucer and ladle are used. Ganges water is poured from one in to the other. At certain sacred seasons a mud image is placed in the saucer to represent Śiva. This is laved with water, and the emblem is a phallic one, but it is doubtful if the women have any idea of its significance.

When anyone decides to take the mantra, her horoscope is examined and the auspicious moment for the ceremony decided. It may be remarked here that in a great many private concerns nothing is done without consulting the stars that rule each destiny. After the initiation, and not till then, does the religious life of a woman formally begin. The only worship in which she is entitled to take part before initiation is Siva pūjā, which may be performed even by little girls. Śiva presides over the marriage fortunes of girls, and can alone grant the boon of

[1] There is a profound belief in the East in the magic of the uttered word.

a good husband and nuptial happiness. A woman cannot even tell her beads until she has received her mantra.

It is held, however, that woman requires no other religion than devotion to her husband, who is for her an incarnation of God. "For woman there is no separate sacrifice, nor vow, nor even fast. If a woman obeys her husband, by that she is exalted in heaven."[1] "Though of bad conduct, or debauched, or even devoid of (good) qualities, a husband must always be worshipped as a god by a good wife."[2]

Worship of the husband includes feet-washing and making obeisance at his feet, regarding the food left on his plate as *prasāda* (consecrated), and eating it as sacramental. The husband is *parama guru*, that is, the chief guru. Even in the presence of the guru, who is regarded as a divinity, the husband must take first place for the wife. The present generation tends to ignore and neglect these practices. A wave of scepticism seems to be passing through Hindu society and affecting even the women, many of whom no longer keep the old routine of piety. But at any moment a woman may suddenly become possessed with a craze for the old ways, and begin observing them with scrupulous exactitude and even passion.

Many women, while accepting this teaching as to the sanctity of the husband, desire a form of worship different from mere wifely duty and devotion. It is not until after marriage that a woman can be initiated by the guru, and in the case of a great many women the ceremony is put off till middle or even old age, because their household duties make it impossible for them to fulfil the demands of religion in the way of bead-telling and meditation. Many women say: "We do not call on God. We have no time."

[1] *Manu*, v. 155. [2] *Manu*, v. 154 (Burnell's Translation).

This probably means that they have not been initiated, and so have no recognized periods of time which they may claim as a right for prayer.

Such prayer, when observed, goes by the name of "remembrance" and "meditation." It is not really thinking or reflecting, but the repetition of the mantra until an image is called up in the mind, and then a fixing of the mind on this image. It involves a relaxation of ordinary attention to one's surroundings, which is supposed to induce the religious mood. But, apart from this kind of prayer, Hindus use ejaculatory prayer in times of danger. This takes the form of repetition of the names of Hari and Nārāyaṇ. Last night, the writer's sleep was broken about three a.m. by a voice that passed along the street, crying out with mournful emphasis, "Hari, Hari, Kṛishṇa, Kṛishṇa, Hari, Kṛishṇa, Kṛishṇa, Hari."

A woman who has "no time" for special prayers can always fall back on the religion of all good women—husband worship. That this is not a mere figure of speech is proved by the fact that many women, after the death of their husbands, make a shrine in his memory and use it as their private oratory. "This is all my life, all my devotion, all my worship," said one such widow devotee to me recently, pointing to a little dais in a room set apart, on which rested her dead husband's photograph, reclining on small cushions, the imprint of his feet taken at his death in red lac on a canvas cloth and mounted, framed, and garlanded with flowers; his pattens, shoes, pipe, walking-stick, brass rice plate,[1] and sundry other intimate belongings. These were arranged on and around the tiny altar with the same meticulous care as is lavished on the idol, and to these she made her daily offering of flowers and holy water, etc.

[1] This plate is really a sacramental vessel, *vide supra*, p. 110.

Perhaps to the impious onlooker there might have occurred an irresistible suggestion of Mrs. Gummidge, whose "thinking of the old un" was so unnerving an emotion. As one looked at the picture of a corpulent and complacent old man, and the childish collection of paltry belongings, one was torn between a sense of the ridiculous and the sublime: on the one hand the unworthiness of the symbol of divinity, and on the other the devotion and tenderness lavished on it by a broken-hearted old woman. One could not consider trivial or untouched by sublimity the tears that coursed down the woman's face as she displayed these objects of her daily worship. Perhaps one of the chief attractions of such worship is that it requires no priest and no cost in money beyond the trifling sum to purchase flowers.

The cost and time involved in religious ceremonial make it difficult for poor or busy people to have it conducted in their homes. In consequence of this, many Hindus content themselves with a daily salutation at the temple. Such salutations are often extremely perfunctory, but the total neglect of worship is unusual. In the case of the women who cannot go to the public shrine, there is often no religious ordinance at all, except an occasional visit to a neighbour's house, where worship is formally conducted and where she may slip in to look on or salute the image. She may not repeat the Vedic mantras which are sacrosanct and forbidden to women. Another reason why pūjā is not conducted in some homes is that they are rented houses and have no special sacredness. The family Lares and Penates are in the ancestral home, and attended there by the hereditary priest, so it is not considered necessary to set up a shrine in a mere rented house.

The lighting of lamps at night has a religious significance.

The lamp is carried by the housemother through each room for *maṅgala*, i.e. good-luck. This may be a survival of a primitive method of scaring away evil spirits.[1] Before the morning and evening worship, mustard seed is scattered before the shrine, to drive away evil spirits who might otherwise make the worship ineffectual.

A favourite deity of Bengali women is Shashṭhī, the protectress of women and children and the presiding genius of healthy maternity. She may be worshipped with or without an image, and the worship can be conducted without a priest. Barren women make offerings and prayers to her. Sometimes she is represented by a banyan twig stuck in a lump of clay, to which artificial flowers, made of sola pith, are offered. In Bengal the worship consists in walking through a wood. At Kālīghat, in Calcutta, may be seen a tree from which are suspended by hairs pieces of brick, fastened there by women who have asked for the boon of a son and promised to pay some vow when the boon is granted. The tree is sacred to Shashṭhī, and is a silent and touching witness to the longing of many sad hearts in Bengal. Shashṭhī-worship is a happy rite, as a rule, and the baskets of "popped" rice sometimes offered are afterwards distributed to children. The goddess, who is represented as riding on a cat, is in some parts of the country identified with Śītalā, the smallpox goddess, who rides on an ass.

Still another festival peculiar to women is *Itu pūjā*, or sun-worship. It is celebrated by filling earthen vessels with certain grains, radish, vermilion, palm sugar, etc. Prayers are then made to the sun for the fulfilment of wishes, and the pots, after being kept for a month, are sunk in a river or pond. It is really a sort of harvest festival, and can hardly

[1] The conches are blown when lamps are lighted.

be dignified with the name of pūjā, whatever its origin may have been. A reason offered to explain sun-worship so late in the year is that during the month the sun is called *Mitra* (friend) and is more likely to give gifts.[1]

The sacred Ganges is for the women a way of holiness. Any morning, in Calcutta, those who are abroad early enough may meet old women, chiefly widows, returning home from the river. In one hand they carry a brass vessel full of the holy water, which is used for sprinkling the places for eating and worship; in the other a little bag, in which the hand holding a rosary is concealed and in which the fingers may be seen to move busily while the mantra is mentally repeated. Their lips do not move but their faces wear an absorbed air, and one knows that the rhythm of their footsteps marks the repetition of the secret formula. Usually the women walk in companies, but single file and silent. There is something heroic in this morning pilgrimage, between dark and dawn, made fasting, and in the plunge of these frail and aged women into the cold and turgid waters of the Ganges. Such women return, not to rest, but often to a day of hard toil. Hinduism is not easy for anyone who takes it seriously.

Lakshmī, the goddess of prosperity, is the deification of the ideas of thrift, order, and the wise use of nature's gifts, and there is a grace in the thought of her blessing a household. The good housewife is called *Bāṛīr Lakshmī*, the kind goddess of the home. A good girl is *Lakshmī meye*, a child amenable to the spirits of good humour and discipline, which make for household peace. There is nothing degrading in such conceptions. They are the primitive attempt to fix an idea in a form that inhabits home and

[1] The sun has a different name each month of the year.

KALIGHAT TEMPLE, CALCUTTA.

Where the Durga Puja is celebrated with great splendour.

Early morning during Durga Puja; women returning from bathing in the sacred water of the Hooghly.—*See description on page 114.*

field—the spirit of happy home-life, not abstractly but concretely conceived. The view of the Hindu woman's religious consciousness must be kept in mind.

While alive to the dangers and degrading tendencies of idolatry, of which history gives examples in plenty, anyone living among a people for whom ideas thus readily become materialised in symbols, or personified in supernatural beings, cannot fail to recognize that much of this symbolism and personification is innocent, and would seem almost inevitable for people at a certain stage of growth. The pity is that the more advanced sections of the race leave the masses without any opportunity to advance from this stage. Many of the gods of popular Hinduism are not far removed in character from the good and bad fairies and the ogres and dragons of universal folklore. To blot out this world of sprites before the mind has learned to conceive of good and bad qualities as disembodied principles, is to leave the ignorant almost without a method of conceiving ideas as realities, and the result is bewilderment. It is only by a gradual and steadfast substitution of heavenly things for the "patterns of things in the heavens" and of truth for the "figures of the true" that man rises to spiritual maturity. The tendency among Hindu philosophers is to leave the immature for ever to their immaturities.

These lines of Francis Thompson picture the world as it must appear to many a simple soul in India:

> "More creatures lackey man
> Than he has note of: through the ways of air
> Angels go here and there
> About his businesses: we tread the floor
> Of a whole sea of spirits: evermore
> Oozy with spirits ebbs the air and flows
> Round us, and no man knows.
> Spirits drift upon the populous breeze
> And through the twinkling leaves that twirl on summer trees."

The poet's fancy is fact for the untutored mind, not only in India but among the untaught peasantries of Russia, or, nearer home, of Ireland, and, until recently, of the Highlands and Hebrides of Scotland. But Francis Thompson in one of his essays shows that sophisticated paganism is a very different thing from the childlike beliefs of the untaught mind, and tends always to degeneration. One finds both types of paganism in India.

For the illiterate, including women, Hinduism makes some provision of religious instruction in the institution of kathakas, accredited reciters of the sacred epics. These kathakas are invited by Hindus who can afford to pay for them, to conduct readings of the scriptures, sometimes lasting for a month or longer, in their houses. In a house known to me, belonging to a wealthy widow, such recitations were paid for at the rate of six hundred rupees a month (about forty pounds), with costly presents of brass, cloth and food. To have the scriptures so read is a means of acquiring merit. The householder and his family have the benefit and pleasure of the reading and explanations, and the neighbours are invited to share in these. In this way, either by hearing or by hearsay, a knowledge of the stories and teachings of the religious epics and Puranas is widely diffused, and the whole speech of the people is coloured by allusions to the story of Rāma and Sītā, the childhood of Kṛishṇa, Sāvitrī who overcame the power of Yama, the god of death, by her wifely devotion, and others. Certain wandering mendicants also collect alms by singing songs about these sacred heroes and about Dūrgā and the god Śiva. Conduct has constant reference to the ideals contained in these stories.

The sacred books, although not called "devatā," receive almost divine honours, and are practically worshipped by Hindus. The śāstras are garlanded at the great festivals, and treated like the images. Even ordinary books are treated as symbols of Sarasvatī, the goddess of learning, and if a book is dropped, or inadvertently injured in any way, it is lifted to the brow by way of salute and apology. This is a custom that has always struck me as very gracious. It is to be regretted that the care does not extend to the ordinary handling of books. Very few Indians are particular to keep books spotless and unmarked by fingers.

Women are not allowed to hear or read the Vedic texts. Indeed, until recent times there has been a rooted objection to woman's learning to read at all. Even at the present day, except among the more progressive sections of Hindu society, a superstition exists that book learning may be a curse to a woman like the forbidden fruit in the Garden of Eden, and may cause widowhood and other disasters. The recitations described above are not a regular part of the women's lives, and some have never listened at all to such readings. Generally speaking, women receive no systematic instruction of a religious kind. The head of a household does not look upon himself as responsible for giving such instruction. "Why do you waste your time trying to teach these womenfolk about spiritual things? They have only the understanding of beasts," was said to the writer once by a villager.

Yet, in considering the religious life of the woman, we must take into account the part played in it by the guru, or religious preceptor.[1] Religious instruction means to us doctrinal and ethical teaching, but the work of the guru cannot be so described. It is the prescribing of ritual and formulæ. For the Hindus, as for the peoples of the ancient world, religion is not primarily a matter of articles

[1] The guru is the official representative of a sect.

of faith or a code of abstract ethics ; it is a rule of behaviour in relation to the family and caste.[1] Consequently, would-be Hindu reformers simply cease to be Hindus, for this rule of life *is* Hinduism. They make a complete breach with the accepted mode of life for the orthodox, and are outcasted.

"The guru is as a father, and the disciple is as a daughter": this popular saying defines the relation of women to their religious teacher, whose main duty to his disciples consists in teaching them how to take their part in the household ritual; the formula to be used in telling their beads ; and the name of the god in particular on whom they are to meditate and whose help they are to invoke daily. Because the guru alone has the power of imparting the *great secret*—the name of the god who is the means of salvation to the disciple—he is himself regarded as divine, and is worshipped daily in his absence by means of symbols, and at his coming is treated as if he were a god.

The guru is supposed to pay periodic visits to the houses of his disciples. His office is hereditary, and father hands on to son the "goodwill" of his group of *śishyas*, or disciples. The visit may be an annual one or more frequent, but it is always regarded as a great occasion. The women of the household wash the guru's feet. The water used becomes sacred and conveys blessing to the disciples, who touch their head and lips with it. It is an exaggeration to say that the water is drunk by the disciples, but sometimes excess of devotion causes strange exhibitions of zeal.[1]

The guru is worshipped by all those who have "taken

[1] Dr. J. N. Farquhar tells of a sect that eats and drinks the excreta of its guru, and at his death drinks water in which the ashes of his cremated body have been mingled. (*Modern Religious Movements in India*, p. 170.)

their mantra." He is then feasted, and the food he has touched becomes sacramental (prasāda), and is eaten as a sacred thing by the disciples. After the guru has been worshipped and feasted, he may or may not give religious teaching. More usually he does not. Any teaching he may give, as far as one may gather from the opinion of intelligent Hindus, is perfunctory and conventional. But the disciple is satisfied that the mere act of listening is a means of acquiring merit.

Besides the hereditary family gurus, there is a certain class of Siddhapurusha, or perfected men who have attained to the status of gods by means of Kālī worship and ascetic practices. They are supposed to be possessed of supernatural powers. Some people become the disciples of such gurus in preference to their household guru, and receive their mantra in this way. These gurus do not teach.

The majority of gurus in Bengal are Tāntrik, i.e. worshippers of the female counterparts of the gods, Kālī, Dūrgā, etc., whose scriptures are the Tantras. In the ancient writings the title of guru was given only to teachers of the Vedas, and only Brāhmans and the other "twice-born" castes could be their disciples. But in modern times, Śūdras and women "were made eligible" for non-Vedic mantras. This has called into being a new type of guru, and vastly increased the scope and power of these persons. But it is only those gurus who refuse to have any but Brāhmans as disciples who are really respected by Brāhmans.[1]

It is a strange fact that, although the temple-priests who serve the household shrine for a monthly fee, and are

[1] For an account of modern gurus, cf. *Hindu Castes and Sects*, J. N. Bhattacharya, pp. 27 ff.

considered absolutely essential to orthodox practice, receive, formally at least, high honour in Hindu households, they are at the same time despised. "Whatever the reason, the priest has a very inferior position in Hindu society."[1] "No Brāhman who could live otherwise would willingly perform the work of a priest."[1] The duties of the idol servers who decorate the idol are regarded as menial, and they are usually ignorant of all but the formalities necessary for the shrine. There is, however, a higher order of priests[2] who officiate at the great festivals. These are held in honour.

The ease with which men may be deified among Hindus is evident even at the present day. One hears occasionally of the formation of small sects having as their leader or object of worship some so-called guru who, by occult or other means, gains a mysterious sway over his followers. They are mostly Kālī worshippers. The writer knew personally a woman whose husband belonged to one such sect. His wife was made the object, the victim rather, of indescribable rites. She contrived to run away. In another case we found in a house a woman completely under the influence of some drug. She had just returned from a shrine where the worshippers, mostly women, were instructed by the *mahanta*[3] to offer this drug to the goddess and then eat it. We were informed that undesirable practices between priest and women went on under this guise, but we had no means of proving the truth of this statement, which, however, was made by respectable Hindu women. A quotation from a well-known book appears to bear out such rumours of shrines dedicated to wickedness. "The neurotic hysteria, which underlies the seeming passivity of many Bengalis, has also led to the creation of small sects, in which worship, whatever its esoteric meaning, appears to

[1] Op. cit., p. 25. [2] The Vedic *āchārya*. [3] Temple attendant.

verge on sexual mania."[1] In a land where insanity is very often not recognized for what it is, and where but little provision is made for the care and cure of the insane, this is perhaps not to be wondered at.

Such depraved forms of worship are ignored by self-respecting Hindus, who are rather apt to think that to treat a fact as if it were not, delivers them from all responsibility regarding it. But in spite of being ignored, there is no doubt of the existence of such sects at the present day, even in Calcutta. "The whole cult is very obscure, partly because it enjoins the strictest secrecy."[2]

One can usually get an honest Hindu to admit this. The writer was told by a Bengali of the carrying on of very objectionable rites, in a house not far from his own, in the north end of Calcutta. When asked why his pārā (section of the town) did not put a stop to it, his reply was: "We respectable Hindus have nothing to do with such people."

Such is the outward framework and background of the Bengali woman's formal religion: "A round of mere external performances, unrivalled in any country for their minute and exacting character."[3] But in actual contact with the pardānaśin, when conversation turns on religion, as it almost invariably does, it is not of these daily practices or the periodic occurrence of feasts and fasts, visits of the guru or visits to the temple, bathings or pilgrimages, that one hears most; not even of the scriptures and their teaching. By some strange paradox, and in direct contradiction, it would seem, to what one might expect from a religion so concrete in its expression, so rigidly conven-

[1] *Bengal, Bihar, and Orissa*, L. S. S. O'Malley, p. 207.

[2] *Bengali Religious Lyrics, Sākta*, E. J. Thompson and A. M. Spencer, Introduction, p. 10.

[3] *Religions of the East*, Alfred S. Geden, M.A., D.D., p. 409.

tional in its usages, thought seems to circle continually, not around the visible and familiar objects and elements of worship, but around certain ever-present and all-controlling *ideas*. And, what is more astonishing to the listener, who comes prepared to hear of a bewildering multitudinousness of gods and goddesses, it is of *God* that Hindus, both men and women, both learned and ignorant, speak; saying simply "He," or referring to Him as Parameśwar, the great god, or Paramātmā, the great spirit. As Sir T. W. Holderness expresses it: "He may worship many gods, demons, and deified heroes; but he dimly believes that they are part of the great unity. In his actual observances he may be classed as a polytheist, one who has many gods; but mentally he is a pantheist, one who sees God in everything. Sitting under a *pipal* (or 'sacred-fig') tree, the present writer has heard a peasant say, 'Parameśvar (the lord of all) is in this tree; he is in the root; he is in the leaves; he is everywhere in the world.'"[1]

The very same belief was expressed to me by a Bengali woman, who said: "He is everywhere," and striking the doorpost, she added: "Even if I say he is in this doorpost, verily it is he, and I must worship it." Polytheism sometimes appears in the light of an attempt to catch this suffused presence and hold it, as a boy catches the sunlight in a piece of mirror glass and makes it play upon his surroundings.

"He is one." No saying is more often heard among thoughtful Bengali women than this, when the subject of modes of worship is referred to; "It is but the ways of approach that differ." Among Hindus themselves the ways are many and varied. From such conversations one gains the impression that even to the women, unversed as they

[1] *Peoples and Problems of India*, T. W. Holderness, p. 114.

are in Hindu theology or philosophy, the main tendencies of Indian thought have somehow filtered through. It is not easy to discover the channels through which these ideas have entered. There is a mass of vernacular religious literature and oral tradition, familiar to the common folk but little known to the foreign student. These are held lightly as subjects of study by Hindu pandits. Such are the lyrics of Chaṇḍī Dās, Rāmprasād Sen, and many others and all the songs and writings that have gathered round the Chaitanya cult. At a later date the life and teachings of Rāmkṛishṇa Paramhaṁsa and Vivekānanda have made the *Bhagavad Gītā* familiar in a way it had never been to the bulk of the people, and have left echoes that one hears in almost every home. Such writings, songs and teachings hold a place similar to revival hymnology, Bunyan's *Pilgrim's Progress*, *The Imitation of Christ*, *The Shorter Catechism*, and other familiar manuals of Christian doctrine or devotion, if not in the character of their influence, at least in its extent and popularity.[1]

Many attempts have been made to sum up in a word or a phrase this twofold character of Hinduism. "Magic tempered by metaphysics,"[2] is one such effort. But epigram seems out of place when one is faced with the great travail of India's past and present to bring forth a thought of reality that satisfies the longing soul of wise and simple alike. Sometimes it seems as if she were drowned in the depth of her own thought, and incapable of return to the surface on which the common life of man is lived.

Some of the oft-repeated words referred to above and the ideas for which they stand are: *Bhakti*, loving devotion to

[1] Cf. *Bengali Religious Lyrics*, *Sākta*, E. J. Thompson and A. M. Spencer.

[2] *The Laws of Manu* (Burnell's Translation), Introduction, p. 3.

a chosen manifestation of God, usually Kṛishṇa; *Karmaphal*, the fruit of the sum total of past lives and their deeds; *Kapāl*, fate; *Mukti*, deliverance from the necessity of rebirth; *Svārtha tyāga*, self-abnegation, which seems to be used in the mystical sense of losing one's self in the divine as also in the more ethical sense of forgetting desire and living the round of duty, sorrow and joy with detachment. The word does not seem as a rule to carry the meaning of self-sacrifice in the service of others, except incidentally. Even service of others may, they think, become too much of an intoxication, and dull one's hunger for God. A Hindu woman was surprised when I spoke of service of her household as work for "others." "They are 'own' not 'other'," she said, expressing a rather fine ideal. She saw no special virtue in toiling for her own.

The chief longing in all Indian hearts in which a religious craving has awakened, is for undisturbed meditation, for escape from mere duty and the service even of loved ones and the giving of undivided time, attention, love, and adoration to "Him." The preaching of a social gospel to such souls falls on deaf ears. They admit that service—"works"—is one way of pleasing God; but there is no rapture in it. To love any human being detracts from the love of God. What is left, when you have loved and served your own or others, is but a poor remnant of your love to offer to Him. Caste feeling has no doubt restricted the development of a sense of obligation to society in general.

Worship even at temples is really individual and not congregational. Each is intent upon his own prayer or offering. "Family" religion also has this solitary character. A woman sits alone, telling her beads and breathing the mantra of her secret god, while all around her are the clatter and indifference of the household. This mood alone—the desire of the mystic for absorbed meditation on the *One*—is recognized as worthy of being counted the highest form of the religious life. Such a belief has been expressed to me again and again, by women as well as men. I have striven, in what I have said above, to derive impressions only from what has actually been said to me by Hindus themselves, not from text-books on Hinduism. This conviction, that all other ways are lesser ways and cannot lead to complete *moksha*,[1] gives rise to a weary restlessness, a sense of cruel bondage, and a profound pessimism. A Hindu writer says on this subject: "Everyone is anxious to get rid of the present condition of life for a better one hereafter. This will be found to be the guiding rule of life of every Hindu, high and low, learned or unlearned. The practical result of this is a spirit of renunciation, of self-denial, of distaste for the things of this world, seldom found in any other people of this world. It has its dark side, too, in the shape of neglect of worldly advancement."[2]

The thought of *māyā* is no mere academic conception. It works with corroding effect upon the daily life of a multitude of souls in India. In her moments of what she believes to be insight, a Hindu woman pities herself for her absorption in family affection, calling it a net, a snare, an intoxication, an illusion, designed to tie her soul to earth and make impossible that moksha, or escape from re-birth, which she desires, and defeating the aim of all her religious practices.

Although this mood does sometimes manifest itself in a dignified stoicism, its result in general is not that hardihood of the spirit that is supposed to be derived from "going all the way with the pessimists." It produces rather a passive resignation and inertia, or else a curious temper which

[1] Deliverance—salvation. [2] *What is Hinduism?* p. 17.

appears to indicate unspoken and sometimes articulate enmity against the gods, or contempt for them. This temper is exceedingly difficult to diagnose, but one hears it expressed, and it appears in popular religious literature. The idea seems to be, that, since the gods show no disposition to make the way of salvation easier for their devotees, since they can neither be persuaded nor cajoled into granting prayers, they must be circumvented, hoodwinked, and defeated.[1] Such is really the *motif* underlying the much-admired story of Sāvitrī, who, by her persistence and shrewdness, as much as by her love of her husband, caught the god of death napping, as it were, and won from him the concession of her husband's life. In a recent book on Bengali religious poetry, the writer says: "The vast Sākta literature is monotonous with its four or five themes—Kālī's neglect of her votary, Śiva's carelessness, the poet's threatened lawsuits or desertion of the mother" (i.e. Kālī).[2]

Even the mantra has in it the idea of a spell by which the god may be in a sense made subject to the will of the worshipper, and the use of meaningless syllables seems to contain a veiled slight to the god. In folktales one also finds the same idea present, for the Brāhman is sometimes able to get the better of the god by his superior wit and cunning.

The meek and longsuffering character of the Indian woman is certainly traceable in part to her belief in

[1] This idea underlies such common practices as letting a boy's hair grow long to make the gods mistake him for a girl, a girl being less likely to cause them jealousy; and the giving of ugly names, expressive of worthlessness, to children, so that the gods may not be tempted to take them away.

[2] *Bengali Religious Lyrics, Sākta*, E. J. Thompson and A. M. Spencer, p. 24.

fate, but her pessimism is not wholly due to this nor to philosophical despair; it has an equally fertile source in the universal fear of malignant spirits, evil omens, curses, and spells by human or superhuman agencies. Indeed, some of the more popular gods are little better than demons, and their worship is wholly propitiatory. The consciousness of a Hindu woman *vis-à-vis* the horrific image of Kālī, whom she fondly addresses as "Mā," is matter for speculation. Alongside of this apparently tender emotion one has to set other feelings expressed in Kālī worship. Her help is invoked by worshippers whose lives are dedicated to robbery, assassination and other violent and anti-social pursuits. This double mood of faith in its meaning of trust in a beneficent power, and fear imploring mercy, is expressed in some of the best-known popular hymns. Sometimes the worshipper is a child clinging to Kālī the mother, and imploring her to be merciful as well as terrible, and to use her bloodstained weapons, not to destroy, but to defend, her child. Again we find an ecstatic glorification of her blood-thirsty aspect, which exercises a morbid fascination. This mood is fruitful in fanatical and sometimes criminal deeds. Again the songs seem to taunt the goddess, crying shame on her blood-thirstiness, on her wild dance, her ogreish appearance, an attitude that leads to cynicism and despair. In the worship of Kālī, the most popular in Bengal, two contradictory elements appear to exist side by side. The contradiction does not seem to disturb the mind of the Hindu, but to reasoned thinking it is impossible to believe that any mind can accept black and white simultaneously and call them the same. Such a state of mind, if it can and does exist, is baffling and unfathomable.

I have not attempted to co-ordinate the external and internal aspects of Hinduism. One is sometimes tempted to think that they are two separate religions or kinds of religion that have no real connection, a higher and a lower thought that met and clashed in the past ages, and then decided to make the peace and exist side by side in a kind of armed neutrality. The grosser forms of Hinduism are sometimes accounted for as being the natural reaction from a pantheism that leads to negation, and the abstractions of "higher" Hinduism as a revolt from the childishness of its concrete forms.

Faced in Corinth with a bewilderment almost as great as one feels at the present day in Bengal, St. Paul wrote: "For though there be that are called gods, whether in heaven or on earth; as there are gods many and lords many; yet to us there is one God, the Father, of whom are all things and we unto him; and one Lord, Jesus Christ, through whom are all things, and we through him. Howbeit in all men there is not this knowledge."

India turns instinctively to human saviours.[1] From Rāma to Rāmakṛishṇa she has looked to see the deity manifesting itself in a perfect man. The great Christian converts from Hinduism have shown a passionate devotion to the personal redeemer, and it may be that India shall find the end of all her spiritual travail when she pours her treasures of bhakti, of loving devotion, upon the Holy One, the All-great who is the All-loving too.

"The more I win Thee, Lord, the more for Thee I pine;
  Ah, such a heart is mine.
My eyes behold Thee and are filled, and straightway then
  Their hunger wakes again!

[1] "Discontent has been frequently expressed with a God who is merely impersonal. 'The worship of the impersonal laid no hold upon my heart,' says Tulsidas, and he is but echoing the feelings and interpreting the practice of multitudes . . ." (*Pantheism and the Value of Life*, W. S. Urquhart, p. 700).

Thou dwell'st within my heart. Forthwith anew the fire
Burns of my soul's desire.
Lord Jesus Christ, Beloved, tell, O tell me true,
What shall Thy servant do?"[1]

[1] From a poem of Nārāyaṇ Vāman Ṭiḷak, a Maratha Christian poet (translated by N. Macnicol).

CHAPTER VII

CHANGES AND THE FUTURE

In a "lament" recently composed in Bengali, these are the opening words: "Bengal was once the home of Bengalis; it is no longer so." The poet himself, explaining the lines to me, said: "The inhabitants of this land do not now speak the Bengali tongue; they do not wear Bengali clothes; they do not eat Bengali food nor follow Bengali customs. All, all is changed." The speaker was not a "nationalist" nor a "swarājist," but simply an old-fashioned Hindu, who loved the ways of his fathers.

The previous chapters have dealt with a static Bengal; with customs and manners that have continued for ages unchanged, and still remain unchanged in many homes, even in Calcutta. But there is a large and always increasing section of society that would not acknowledge the foregoing descriptions as applying to itself, except in some external aspects. And it is not only among those who have broken away definitely from caste and orthodoxy, but throughout the educated community as a whole, that many changes are manifest, both outward and beneath the surface. The young man of today in Bengal talks glibly of "suffering from transition," as if it were some sort of epidemic; but even in the quiet backwaters of the inner court this changing state of things is "sensed." A thoughtful pardānaśin remarked to me recently: "The events that we see about us nowadays are the signs of an age about to pass away."

There was a note of death rather than of renaissance in her words, uttered gravely and sadly. With the conservatism of the Hindu, she loved what was old and familiar, and feared what was new and unknown. To her mind change spelt decay and not progress.

In tracing some of these changes and striving to discover their cause and meaning, it is easy to stray from the region of facts in the direction of mere private opinion. An attempt will be made to stick to facts which can be tested by any observer; but some expression of personal views and some forecasting of the future, are almost unavoidable as one considers the present-day position of the Bengali women of the bhadra-lok class.

Sixty years ago the women of India did not know they were not as free as it is possible for self-respecting women to be. If they had ever heard of freedom, they neither admired it nor desired it. They know today that they are not free, even although they reveal their knowledge of the fact, not so much by brooding over their own unfree condition as in saying to women of other races: "You are free"; and in contemplating the freedom of others, which has for them a curious fascination not unmixed with dread. The majority of pardānaśins, if offered unconditioned social freedom tomorrow, would refuse it, because they would not know what to do with it. Some Christian women, for instance, have never really discarded the veil except in a very slight degree—e.g. when present at church. One sympathises with this attitude, in so far as it shows an unwillingness to create too great a gulf between their own community and the older communities.

The idea of freedom as a possibility for Indian women is now present in many minds. And when I use the word "freedom" it is in contrast to "seclusion," and does not imply that Indian women are prisoners and captives, but simply that they have never taken part in social life outside the walls of their home, nor in any sort of public life as long as they have remained orthodox Hindus. In the house of a rājā I heard the senior rānī remark: "What's going to happen now? Who knows? Anything may happen, since the Mahārānī of X has discarded pardā, for of all aristocratic and conservative Hindu families they were the strictest."

The occasion of this remark was an evening "party," given in honour of some official. It was strange to see, in one part of the house, the lavish entertainment of Europeans, their women, in full evening dress, chatting to the men of the house under glittering electric lights, while behind the scenes, in a room simple to bareness, sat the chief lady of the mansion, cross-legged on a low wooden seat, surrounded by her daughters-in-law and maidservants, and unable to exchange a word with her guests, both for reasons of propriety, in the case of the men, and through ignorance of English on her part, and the vernacular on their part, in the case of the women—except one or two who happened to know Bengali. Is it surprising that in minds such as hers the ferment should be at work, or that she should partly hate and partly long for the freedom that makes it possible for other women to invade her house and flaunt their charms before the husband, in whose presence she has always veiled her face except in solitude?

The mutual attraction and repulsion of races makes them imitate each other, not always as the sincerest form of flattery, but quite as often as the surest means of self-defence. M. Anatole France makes one of his flippant Alexandrians in *Thaïs* remark to a Christian ascetic: "Latin wisdom ought, in fact, to admit your Christ into our pantheon. It was a maxim of our forefathers that there was something divine in every god." But it was the defence of the pantheon against the encroachments of Christianity, rather than the glory of the Church, that the prefect had in mind when he made this concession to the Christian monk. In some such spirit the East frequently adopts social and political innovations from the West.

There are many Bengalis who might truthfully give expression to their real inner convictions in some such words as the following: We are better than Europeans, more intellectual, more spiritual; but they enjoy certain temporary and merely adventitious qualifications which give them, for the time being, and in the world as at present constituted (this being the black age for us Hindus), considerable advantages over us. Let us but acquire these chance qualities and assets, and our position will then become, not only in reality as it now is—for are not we the truly twiceborn—but in appearance also, so that all men shall know it, equal to, and indeed superior to, theirs. Let us remove our accidental handicaps and the world is ours—spiritually. One of the most obvious of these handicaps is the regrettable position of woman in India. "Can man be free if woman be a slave?" wrote Shelley, and the question forms part of India's heart-searchings at this moment.

"The degradation of our women has rebounded upon the men, bringing adequate punishment for their inequity. The birth of a female child is universally bewailed as a misfortune. . . . It is meet that we should pause to consider the loss of energy that this order of things is entailing upon our society. . . . On account of want of harmony of education in the male and female sections of our society, our domestic and social life has become a scene of discord and unhappiness, and this has proved an insurmountable obstacle to our social progress." Such a passage, taken from the newspaper report of the presidential address at a recent Bengal Social Conference, the speaker being a Hindu, expresses the now generally acknowledged fact that Bengali society is sadly handicapped by this state of things.

The remedy is by no means as easy as it might seem to an onlooker, who would say: Well, if they feel like that about it, why not set their women free, give them a decent education and be done with it? Sister Nivedita (Miss Noble), reviewing this situation, says very sympathetically and truly, "Under the old scheme, women found not only a training and a discipline, but also a career. It was a preparation and an opportunity fitted only, it is true, to the soil on which it grew. This limitation pervades the whole of the Indian civilization. . . . Some great educational adjustment is necessary at this moment."[1] Dr. Tagore feels the pathos and the danger of his countrywomen's position, and uses it with justification as a symbol of India's bewilderment: "In that future I saw my country, a woman like myself standing expectant. She has been drawn forth from the home corner by the sudden call of some Unknown. She has had no time to pause or ponder, or to light herself a torch, as she rushes forward into the darkness ahead."[2]

Fortunately, this somewhat tragic image of India's behaviour, present or future, has to be tempered by the consideration that up till now Britain, like one of her own burly and benevolent policemen at a London crossing, has caught her gently and firmly by the elbow, and stopped her impulsive career through the traffic of the present age,

[1] *The Web of Indian Life*, Sister Nivedita, p. 81.

[2] *The Home and the World*, Rabindranath Tagore, p. 136.

with the words: "Steady, lady. Just a moment, please, till I get a crossing cleared for you." It will not be the constable's fault if she slips from his detaining grasp and dashes in, taking all the risks.

The difficulty of adjusting her culture to the needs of the new world has sometimes resulted in a stubborn glorification of the past by Indian writers and speakers. It is not India's culture but the age that is out of joint. This is a perfectly natural human reaction. A lady, whose middle-aged figure can in no wise be made to look elegant in the latest craze of fashion, comforts herself by looking at youthful photographs of herself, and tells her juniors how much more womanly and graceful the fashions used to be. Mr. William Archer says in his book, *India and the Future*: "No nation in the world will ever qualify itself for facing the complications of the future by idealising and idolising the past." Hindus should find a belief in, and reverence for, the future in their own śāstras, for is there not a promise that there shall be a period of restoration during the incarnation of *Kālki*? This is a sign that all goodness, according to the Hindu seers, is not in the past, but that, alike with Christian prophecy, they look for a new heaven and a new earth in which dwelleth righteousness.

No attempt can be made here to define in detail the widespread changes that are determining the social, political, and religious future of India as a whole, but only in so far as these affect women and tend to modify the elements in their domestic and social life that have formed their characters and determined their status and outlook. With all due honour to the best type of Hindu woman, it is doubtful if she is fitted to start on the perilous journey of new adventure on which her country has set forth. And yet she cannot be left behind. The right uses of freedom must be taught her while she is still young and pliable, in the home circle, and at school.

Every aspect of life referred to in what has already been written, is being played upon by the new forces now let loose upon India. The old ways go on, but with a difference. Examples often appear trivial, but they are the straw that shows how the wind blows. Take, for instance, fear, which has been one of the controlling factors in the lives of the ignorant masses and of the women of India. Fear centres chiefly in what cannot be understood. Scientific knowledge filters down from educated to ignorant, and robs some old terrors of their power to dismay even the stout-hearted. New knowledge of natural facts has, for example, turned the frenzied blowing of conches during an eclipse into a playful survival. The ancient Hindus, it is true, had understood the true nature of solar or lunar eclipse, but to the average Indian it was the work of a dragon, in whose dark shadow malignant powers had unusual opportunity. For its duration, defilement necessitated bathing in the sacred rivers and regarding as unclean all food cooked previously to the eclipse. Such a view cannot now be seriously taken of a natural phenomenon except by the totally ignorant, although the popular practices continue.

Again, Śītalā, the smallpox goddess, has lost some of her prestige since vaccination has shown that her power can be checked. Modern electric lighting, or even the humbler gas lamp or kerosene lantern, have depopulated the labyrinth of dark Calcutta lanes of their *bhūtas* or evil spirits. The germs of plague or cholera or typhoid may be only a little less terrifying than the demons who used to scatter these evils in their train, but they are now, in some measure at least, amenable to the treatment which modern medical science has discovered, and inoculation and disinfectants are ousting the more picturesque methods of incantation and magic.

Western education, the press, social and religious teaching based on Christian doctrines, travel abroad, telegraphic communication with the rest of the world, the kinema, world flights, and many other material and non-material influences, obvious to anyone with even a slight acquaintance with India or other Asiatic countries, are continually at work, in more or less degree, on Indian minds everywhere. But there are other influences, not so obvious but very potent, that have had a wide-reaching effect upon the sentiment and thought of the people. Such, for example, is India's new interest and participation in Western sports (and especially success in competition with the West), and the new contact, by means of travel and newspapers, with other Asiatic countries like Japan. An Asiatic as well as a national feeling is growing up in India, and the ideals and standards of Asia as a whole are being put in the balance agains European culture.

It cannot be claimed that the women of India are to any extent conscious of, or alive to, these new currents of thought. But it is certain that, indirectly, they are being influenced by them, and that the old orthodox manner of life is vaguely disturbed by all the changes that have shortened distances, dispelled ancient and dreaded ills, turned darkness into light, levelled some of the differences between race and race, and brought the peoples of the world physically and mentally into closer contact, resulting both in new rivalries and clearer mutual understanding. As far as the rural life of Bengal is concerned, recent changes have not been altogether for good. This is due to the familiar phenomenon of the "deserted village," in districts where wealth accumulates in the town and men decay in the hamlet. In earlier days life in India was, with few exceptions, a village life. Even the towns were peopled by those who came from the country, and the towns themselves were like collections of villages, and did not possess a common civic life as it is understood in the West. Families lived on their properties or small holdings of land, and grew and increased there to the size of little clans. In the country towns and villages one still gets a very distinct picture of this kind of life, self-sufficing and self-contained, often to the almost entire exclusion of all but blood relations. But it is passing away. Everywhere one sees change and sometimes ruin. The purely agricultural life, which sustained these communities, is still in evidence, but it is no longer sufficient for the demands made on it by a new standard of living.

It is not necessary here to go into the complicated question of the causes or avoidability of such changes; it is enough for our purpose to note how widespread they have been.

Since the family estate can no longer support the family, the sons have to leave home and seek employment; and, in consequence, these old homes, in which, under former conditions, the whole family resided in moderate prosperity, cannot now be kept up as they used to be. The younger sons go to the cities for education, without which they cannot hope to get employment, leaving their wives and mothers and the older men of the household to carry on a somewhat melancholy existence in the ancestral home. Life in the city gives them a distaste for the dead-and-alive existence of the malaria-infected "mofussil." They get swallowed up by the demands of the town in professional or commercial life, and settle there in rented quarters that tend to become their permanent home, but which have a character quite different from home in the older Indian sense.

When the wife reaches a suitable age, she joins her husband. If he is making money, other members of the family will come to "sponge" on him, and, at last, the once comfortable, dignified country house is left to a few thin widows and decrepit elders, who are driven from one corner to another as the brick and mortar crumble with the swift tropical decay and there is no one left to repair the waste places. This new kind of life is giving the women, as well as the men, an entirely new outlook. They have escaped from much of the pressure of authority and are free as they have never been before. The younger men, more sophisticated and "knowing," if not wiser, than the last generation, are no longer greatly influenced by their elders, whom they regard as too simple to guide them. Yet they are curiously unable to guide themselves, and many of the leaders they follow often prove will-o'-the-wisps.

The wife, living alone, it may be in a rented house, cannot now leave the care of domestic affairs and the management of the purse to older, more experienced hands, but must begin, while she is still young and often quite untaught, to be sole housekeeper and to control the family life. Her domestic staff no longer consists of old family retainers, but more often of expensive and inefficient casual "helps," with none of the filial or paternal attitude towards the young wife which formerly determined the relations of mistress and servant. From observation of this kind of *ménage*, one can only say that, for want of training and experience in the young women, its results are often a pathetic and dismal failure, and are at the root of a good deal of ill-health and misery in Calcutta. The blame is sometimes laid at the door of the very small amount of schooling the girl has had, which (not the smallness but the education) is said to have spoiled her as a housewife. The real causes are not understood nor dealt with. Hindus have not yet grasped the fact that a good education trains a woman in practical capacity; and the notion is rife among them that a knowledge of books gives woman a contempt for household tasks and the care of children. The tidy and hygienic Western home in the same classes is a sufficient answer; but few Indians have opportunities of observing the household ways of Western women.[1] When the Indian wife returns from such conditions to visit her husband's paternal home she does not find it easy, after her comparative freedom, to submit in all things to her mother-in-law. Such submission was formerly the key to the Indian woman's character, and it is easy to imagine what a transformation her new attitude is bringing about, a transformation that is everywhere manifesting itself in Indian life, and for which little preparation is being made by Hindu society.

Even where the joint family still lives on the same plot of ground, there is a marked tendency in the sons, on the death of their father, to divide the family property and break up the old house into separate dwellings. *Bhāi bhāi, ṭhāin ṭhāin* (" As many abodes as there are brothers ") is a proverbial saying nowadays. Such divisions often give rise to bitterness, or else spring from quarrels that are the very reverse of the old Hindu family ideal of having all things in common. The strain and jealousy, so prevalent in private life, are reflected only too plainly in the irritation and quarrelsomeness so evident in the public life

[1] *Vide supra*, p. 47.

of Bengal at the present day. When families divide up in this way, it brings about hardship and distress for the members of the family, not making an income otherwise, whose portion of the joint inheritance is too small to be adequate for a decent style of living. This falls most heavily on the women. Another result of the disruption of family life is that loneliness is added to seclusion in the case of the pardā women. They no longer have the chatter and comradeship of a crowd of women relatives to make the time pass cheerfully. They are harassed by the greater strain of reduced means, and find too burdensome the work of the house and the care of the children, which can no longer be shared. This is particularly hard at the time of childbirth, which was made easy by the rule of the "time of separation" in the family house. Rest and freedom from household toil were thus insured.

Finding themselves alone, the women are obliged to think more than they used to do. Reflection reveals to them some of their own ignorance and inability to manage their own affairs. A Brāhman widow, of aristocratic but impoverished family, so situated, said to me once: "You know what a fool I am. I do not know how to write to you nor even how to speak to you or to anyone. I am a perfect donkey." She had suffered much at the hands of unscrupulous persons because of this simplicity, and felt handicapped and bewildered. Such women naturally wish to establish a more secure and satisfactory relation with the outside world, for they are at the mercy of advisers, who often care nothing at all for the interests of the woman, but only for their own advantage.

In the cities these lonely wives meet other women who have been to good schools and are much more enlightened than themselves. They determine that their daughters shall not be brought up in ignorance as they have been, but in this laudable ambition they often get little encouragement. If the husband is sympathetic, the girls sometimes have a chance of education; but if he is continually worried by the struggle for existence, the strain of the new mode of life, and the thought of the ever-dreaded marriage expenses, the state of the daughters may end by being more pitiable than that of the mothers, for they will have to face a life of even greater difficulty, under disadvantages becoming always more severe.

Some mothers, after a brave start in trying to better matters, become profoundly discouraged by the unfriendliness of society towards their ambitions, and its general unpreparedness for the educated girl. A Bengali lady, married in Bengal, but educated from girlhood in England and a graduate of one of its leading colleges, was heard to vow that her daughter should have none of this higher education, but should be trained in domesticity only, so that she might fit more comfortably into a society in which the truly cultured woman finds herself in a painful isolation.

Miss Cornelia Sorabji,[1] writing in the English Press, gives the following incident from her experience: "A very progressive father married his son, who was to have a thoroughly modern (European) education, to a young girl, and sent her to have her education in Paris. The girl returned some years later to a conventional Hindu household, 'a translation in French.' She spoke nothing but French, she dressed French, even to her shoes.[2] She found herself in a zenana with women of all generations, from a great-grandmother downwards, with none of whom had she a word or thought or ambition in common. The women in their turn were horrified at her. She had none of the

[1] *The Fortnightly Review*, May, 1924. [2] *Vide supra*, p. 97.

attributes of a Hindu bride proper."[1] They proceed to "translate her into the vernacular." "To all of these things she submitted like one from whose body the soul had fled; but they could not make her speak their language in a day, nor in a day could they teach her the worship of her husband—how to cook his food and wait upon him, or the wifely etiquette, how to hide her face in his presence . . . nothing but fear of the head of the family kept the women kind to her." At last the oldest woman asked her what they could do to make her less unhappy. And she, pining for privacy, asked that she might have an hour a week all to herself. "When the wish was granted, she dressed herself in her French clothes, hat and all, and walked up and down the room talking French aloud to herself. . . . You see," adds Miss Sorabji, "that at present reformation is tolerated less than secession." And the writer's conclusion, a very wise one, is: "We must help people, must we not? *at the place where they are.*"

To return to the woman living with her husband in a small rented house, another matter that troubles her is the knowledge that now he needs her companionship far more than formerly, since he no longer has the society of brothers and cousins to make his leisure hours cheerful. She discovers that there are accomplished actresses in the theatres he visits, and that even the women of the streets cultivate their mental as well as their physical charms by learning to read and sing. Schools for Hindu girls sometimes have to deal with applications for admission from the guardians, or owners rather, of girls belonging to undesirable houses, who, almost more than any class at the present moment, are diligent in the pursuit of education and accomplishments.

[1] *Vide supra*, p. 40.

All this makes for restlessness on the part of the helpless pardānaśin. She sees the dangers and embarrassments of her position, and recognizes that it is no longer enough for a Hindu wife to be her husband's domestic slave, however devoted. She longs to be his comrade in a far truer sense, often with a mute love that is pathetic to witness. She compares herself with the women of other races, of whom she catches glimpses through the slats of her closed carriage it may be, and about whom she hears. Whatever she may have been told to the contrary, her woman's instinct tells her that these happy-faced European, Armenian or Parsee mothers are good women, and she begins to believe that freedom is, after all, not an unnatural or dangerous state for women any more than for men. Perhaps she dreams of a day when all the holy beauty that has gathered in the home round the name of mother will become a halo round the name of woman in the wider world, not as mother only, though always chiefly, nor as beloved maiden, though romance will not die because woman is free (it has always been greatest where woman is freest), but as the gentler half of the human race, who can bring into social and national life all that passion of tender service that she has lavished on home and husband and children; for nature has appointed her the giver and guardian of life.

If India had remained where she was a hundred years ago, the emphasis which her domestic and social discipline has laid on the virtues of passivity and submission to authority, might still have served her purpose; but she has changed in great degree her temper and attitude, and is demanding freedom, as it has been understood and practised by the nations of the West. For the uses of such freedom, it is evident that a new type of culture and

KAMALA DEVI

Daughter of the late Sir Asutosh Mookerjee, Kt.,
Vice-Chancellor of the University of Calcutta

character has become necessary for woman no less than man. The isolation of India, an isolation both physical, because of her geographical boundaries, and mental, because of the unique and exclusive nature of her culture, is a thing of the past. Her fortunes have now become inextricably linked with the West and the further East. She is wedged between old and new forces, and if she remains passive she will be crushed. She can resist the outward pressure only by developing pressure from within like the acorn, whose growth splits the rock.

It is the custom among Bengalis to remodel and reset the family jewels for new brides, so that they may be "nuton feshion," as they say. The result sometimes is that beautiful antique ornaments are cast into the melting pot, and the fine old workmanship and curious design are turned into something garish and unbecoming to the beauty of the East. The following slight incident may be taken as a human parallel to this remodelling, regarded as a parable of change. Among my pupils was a beautiful and gracious young Brāhman wife, the product of the best type of Hindu home life. A male member of the household, whose profession necessitated long residence in England, had had his young daughter educated there, and the girl had returned to India the lovely bride of a young Bengali civilian. My shy pupil asked me how she should receive the newcomer, who was expected to pay a visit, though no longer, for reasons of caste, permitted to live in the family house. I enquired as to their relative ages, and the young wife replied, "O, she is older in years, but *in title to honour* I am her superior." This was said quite modestly, and was a reference to the household etiquette of precedence, but there was also a dignity in the remark in which seemed to lurk a protest that mere external things should put her at a disadvantage with her brilliant "inferior in honour." Her attitude is that of many a fine woman of the orthodox classes, conscious that the world which gave her homage is moving away from her. She is slightly on the defensive because sure of the worth of all she has been taught to prize, and yet feels that, somehow, her old-fashioned virtues have little market value in the present-day world.

Change is ever accompanied by some loss, but it is the desire of all those who love India and her women that in the recasting and renewal that seem inevitable, the graces and virtues grown in their cloistered existence may be transformed to even greater beauty and worth, and not lost or destroyed by the rude hand of time. In a letter to me from a young Hindu gentleman, the complaint is made that "the girls are not allowed the opportunity of Western culture, nor do they get native culture, as they have been removed from the soothing and improving atmosphere of joint families in open villages to the self-centred little houses of the big cities. The old ways of the pieties and charities are not observed. The girls are now almost ignorant of the semi-religious *bratas* [vows] and rites."

Although there is a fairly widespread belief in, and desire for, the education of girls, no great effort has yet been made by the people themselves to provide educational facilities, or by the parents to avail themselves of such education as is to be had. In Bengal the number of girls under instruction in schools is still less than two per cent. The reason for this lies chiefly in the fact of the early marriage of daughters, which constitutes such a drain upon the family resources that the parents are either unable or unwilling to make the monetary sacrifices necessary for the additional cost of education. In exceptional cases the relatives of the bridegroom ask for a certain amount of education in a girl, but, generally speaking, they set greater store by the colour of her skin and the size of her dowry. "It is often observed in our society that the relatives of the bridegroom never enquire about the education or character of the bride at the time of selecting her. They want two things only—the golden complexion of the bride and the gold of the father."[1]

The Government Reports, both Provincial and Imperial, repeat the same tale. After all the attempts to get some "way on," the results are lamentably small. "It is difficult to exaggerate the obstacles to the progress of women's education in India. All the influences which operate against the spread of education among boys—the conservatism and prejudice of the people, the remoteness of the advantages accruing from education, the indifferent quality of the education offered and its cost—all gain added strength in opposing the education of girls."[2] Here and there in certain sections of society there is marked advance, but the failure of general progress only serves to make of women who are educated a class apart.

In a collection of stories about Indian marriage, acknowledged by Hindus to be a very accurate picture of family life, a harsh mother-in-law speaks thus of the educated wife her son has chosen: "I shall mend her or end her relationship once and for all, and get another and less learned wife for my son. . . . I shall lick her into shape very soon; I shall make her forget all her booklore and curse the very day on which her precious brother took it into his head to teach her." She speaks of the girl's accomplishments

[1] From a speech by a leading Hindu.

[2] *Eighth Quinquennial Review of Education in India*, vol. i. p. 126.

as suited only to courtesans and "shameless white women."[1]

To change such an environment into one that tolerates the "new woman" of India, is no small part of the task of educationists. The situation of a cultured girl in an illiterate household is bad enough, but more difficult still is the position of the independent wage-earning or professional woman in a society that has no rule for the treatment of such unusual members. Not only is the woman doctor, school-inspectress, or teacher, lonely, but she is suspect. "Apart from the paucity of trained teachers there is another deterring consideration. The educated woman is in any case lonely, and if she is in pardā away from her family, the loneliness must be beyond description, yet if she is out of pardā she often loses respect that is necessary to win scholars. Injudicious appointments of young girls away from their homes have . . . produced a series of disasters calculated to bring female education into disrepute with respectable villagers." Much of the primary education given in rural districts is almost worthless, and has no lasting effect. "These wretched so-called schools do not produce much good result. Most of them are held in a hut or cowshed, or a room or verandah of a ruined or dilapidated house, which is very dangerous. There is often no apparatus and no furniture. The children sit on mats and write with chalk on the floor." Thus writes an Indian lady inspector in Bengal. Yet we have seen excellent work done by trained and conscientious teachers even in such conditions. Enthusiasm is better than furniture.

It must be admitted, however, that the pupils of such schools often lapse back into complete illiteracy. "One of the chief needs of the present day is to improve the quality

[1] *Short Stories*, Kusika.

of the work in primary schools so that more girls may be enabled and encouraged to proceed to a higher stage of education, eventually to return as teachers to the help of their fellow-countrywomen. This improvement must be accompanied by persistent but well-considered efforts to overcome the obstructions offered by conservatism and prejudice. In this work the help of the educated women of India would be invaluable, but the co-operation is needed of all who believe that the education of women is essential to national advancement."[1]

Such efforts towards improvement of girls' education have been made successfully, but on all too small a scale, owing to the limitations of funds and workers, by the Brahmo Samāj and certain Hindu associations that have followed their example ; but most notably and persistently by various British and American missionary societies, who have been the pioneers and chief movers in all private effort on behalf of the education of girls. Of the ten non-Government high schools for girls in Bengal, seven are Mission institutions.[2] "Much is left to Missions," says one of the Government reviews.[3]

Highly trained women, both European and Indian, have braved adverse public opinion and perejudice and even malice, living among the people, often misunderstood and sometimes slandered ;[4] yet by patient work and unfailing

[1] *Eighth Quinquennial Review of Education in India*, vol. i. p. 139.

[2] *Seventh Quinquennial Review of Education in India*, vol. i. p. 172.

[3] *Seventh Quinquennial Review of Education in India*, vol. i. p. 172.

[4] Even European missionaries, as the writer has discovered more than once, are sometimes supposed to be "kept" women. Hindu women find it difficult to believe that without some such arrangement they would not be molested.

friendliness and willingness to help, they have overcome opposition, and, better still, have here and there galvanised the community into establishing rival schools, a not unhealthy result of example.

Girls' high schools are pronounced by officials to be superior to boys' high schools, and the reason given is: "This is partly due to the fact that secondary schools for girls are largely under Mission management." Schools under Indian management are growing in number and efficiency, and most of them are as full as they can hold, and ready to expand but for financial stringency. Government gives what grants it can, but the Education Department has been unable of late years to meet the increasing demands made upon it. The War, and subsequent hard times, have diminished foreign support, and foreign workers have been handicapped personally by the high cost of living in India and the fluctuations of exchange. More and more the progress of education must depend upon Indian effort, which so far has not shown sufficient vigour.

In spite of these difficulties real progress is visible, and there are good grounds for hope that the dark ages are past. Things impossible even ten years ago are now taken as a matter of course.[1]

There are pioneer women everywhere, and a growing confidence in and admiration of the independent women among her fellow-countrywomen. Recently I met a Hindu woman graduate, married to a young college lecturer, who was continuing her work as a teacher in order to make it possible for her husband to go to Europe for further study. Such marriages are still rare, but a very significant sign of

[1] "It is the magnitude of the problem, rather than the lack of effort, which makes the rate of progress seem so painfully slow." (*India in 1924-25*, L. F. Rushbrook Williams.)

the times. "Giving Indian women a chance," a phrase used in the *Fifth Quinquennnial Review of Education in Bengal*, has become a familiar quotation in subsequent reviews and reports. It occurs in the following passage: "The field has been well mapped out, and a comprehensive system has been evolved. . . . Is it too much to hope that we shall be so able to order things that the education given will be a reality? There is only one way of accomplishing this, and that is by securing cultured and sympathetic women to work as inspectresses and in colleges and schools, and by giving these women as free a hand as possible. If we determine to do this and do not shrink from the bill . . . we shall be giving Indian women a chance."

This passage hints at the great difficulty of getting women of good family and character, as well as culture, to be the ambassadors for a new *entente* between the past and the future. The great physical difficulties of travel in Bengal, especially for a solitary woman, and the dangers and temptations to which she is exposed in a society not ready to trust a woman unprotected by a male relative, have, in spite of emoluments and official prestige, deterred many women from volunteering for this work. But this, too, is changing as the numbers increase and Hindu society becomes accustomed to the new phenomenon. In this matter Indian Christian women have been conspicuous. "Indian public opinion is slowly changing from its former attitude of positive dislike to the education of girls, and is progressing through apathy to cordial co-operation," is a hopeful remark in another education review.

One of the recommendations of the Calcutta University Commission, presided over by Sir Michael Sadler, then Vice-Chancellor of Leeds University, was that "an attempt should be made to organise pardā schools for Hindu and Muslim girls whose parents are willing to extend their education to 15 or 16." Schools for caste girls in Calcutta have always had to be more or less pardā for all except the youngest pupils. Of recent years the growing demand for education has put girls' schools on a better financial footing, so that suitable buildings have been put up by private enterprise and adequate conveyance arrangements been provided. In such institutions as Duff School,[1] which stands in the centre of one of the chief Bengali residential quarters and is staffed by European graduates and Indian trained teachers, a curriculum is provided for senior girls, including hygiene, first-aid and nursing, housewifery, music, designing, etc., as well as the ordinary school subjects. Young married women and widows from Hindu households attend these classes. The work is still at the experimental stage, and attendance of the oldest pupils, owing to family claims on their time, apt to be erratic, but it is full of promise and full of interest.

There are now several such schools in Calcutta under the management of various sects, but in the province outside little advance has been made. Of girls attending school in the whole of Bengal, 99 per cent. are at the primary stage. This shows how prevalent still are the customs of early marriage and seclusion of girls. It is gratifying, however, during a quarter of a century in Calcutta, to have been a witness of, and to have had some small share in, the work of those who are breaking down such traditions.

Judged by higher education, the advance is striking. In 1921, as many as forty-five women graduated B.A. from Calcutta University. All of these are, of course, not Bengalis; and of the Bengalis the majority in any year

[1] Under the auspices of the United Free Church of Scotland.

would be Brahmos or Christians; but the existence of a growing class of educated Bengali women is telling unmistakeably on public opinion.

Industrial schools are conducted here and there in Calcutta and other parts of the province, where women may learn silk and cotton weaving, embroidery, lace, and carpet making, and the preparation of condiments and preserves. Missions were the pioneers in this work, and still control the most successful of such institutions for Indian women. The women and girls respond quickly to training and are neat and accurate workers, but lack invention, which is usually supplied by those who train them. The market for the work done is, unfortunately, an artificial one, and the disposal of the products of such schools entails a great deal of effort on the part of the management. The pupils themselves cannot sell their wares. Very often similar work is done in the towns or villages under sweated conditions, and sold at a price which makes experiments in cottage industries mostly infructuous. Government started, some years ago, a depôt for cottage handmade fabrics and metal work, etc., before the *khaddar* cult had been heard of; but the Indian public has not provided many customers. Most of the buyers appear to be Europeans with a taste for "quaint" things.

Political life in India—a new thing in the East—has acted as a spur to the progress of women's education and emancipation. The militant suffrage workers of Europe at first shocked Indian sentiment, and seemed to justify a desire to go back to a more rigid insistence on woman's subordination. But the spirited behaviour of English girls and women during the War, in shouldering the tasks of men, stirred a profound sympathy in the hearts of Indian women. And the consequence of militant tactics (although it is claimed that the vote was a reward for the good behaviour of women during the War), the granting of the suffrage to women, has awakened political ambitions among the advance guard of Indian women, who do not seem to relish the thought of their country's being governed by a Parliament which includes women, unless they, too, are to have a voice in the control of legislation.

Several steps have been made towards political enfranchisement. In Bombay, Madras and Bengal women now have a vote for the Legislative Council.

In 1924 the Calcutta municipal vote was given to women taxpayers, the minimum amount of tax-payment being very low, so that a large number of women are included. At the first municipal election under the new regime in Calcutta, very few women appeared at the polling stations, although elaborate arrangements had been made for their convenience and a great number of women volunteers were present to help them. At a polling station at which I assisted, only one *bona fide* pardānaśin came to record her vote. Her son was one of the members of the Corporation, so presumably she was better informed than others. This enfranchisement is more a men's than a women's movement in India.

More striking than the number of women who took the trouble to record their votes was the large number of educated, English-speaking, Indian women, summoned by the Chairman of the Corporation to assist him in making polling arrangements, and their eagerness to make the venture a success. This is significant of the change that the last few years have made in the outlook and interests of women. Some of the women showed that the capacity for administration as heads of households which the Hindu system demanded of women, was ready to find a larger field, and to prove itself in civic as well as in domestic life.

Social service is an idea that is beginning to make a strong appeal to young men and women in Asia. A young Chinese woman graduate, in the course of an eloquent address in English to an audience of Indian women students recently gathered in Calcutta,[1] said that, among the young people of China who had drifted away from orthodox religion and had adopted no new faith, the words Social Service now stood for religion. The vacuum caused by the loss of belief in ancient tradition and practice, and the inability to embrace to order any new religious convictions, had been filled by an enthusiasm for the salvation of society, by the service of the poor and oppressed, the education of the masses, the liberation of women, and other efforts to improve their country.

Much the same might be said of India at the present day. The most vigorous bodies of reform, such as The Servants of India, put social service and not religious teaching in the forefront of their activities. Some of the outstanding personalities in India, like Mr. Gokhale, and Mr. Gandhi, have derived their chief inspiration from such movements. This trend towards social service on the part of patriotic Hindus constitutes a ground upon which East and West may form contacts mutually pleasant and beneficial. Such a means is now open to women also. There are various ways in which united service of the community may be made a meeting place for Indian and English women, notably such philanthropic work as Child Welfare. During the War, the co-operation of Indian and European women workers created a new sentiment of mutual trust and respect, and

[1] Under the auspices of the Young Women's Christian Association.

everything should be done to maintain the happy relations then established.

European women, from longer practice, are more able as a rule, than Indian women, to organise public work and to carry it on in a disinterested and impersonal spirit. The Indian woman, even when eager to do good for her country, requires the personal motive. She is more ready to devote herself to a person than to a "cause," unless that cause is embodied in a person or persons known to her. But a cause can be made a live thing to her if she is associated in working for it with ardent personal leadership. This is where, it seems at the present time, European women can serve the women of India. The Council of Women in Calcutta is an attempt to gather together the people who are really trying to do something for the community, both Indian and European. Hard, honest work must always win respect and provoke imitation, and women of East and West are learning of each other that neither vision alone, nor practical measures alone, can save society, but a practical mysticism which East and West, working together, may hammer out. The shaper of iron must have glowing heat as well as mighty blows to achieve his ends.

An emancipated Hindu lady said to me recently: "Give me Englishwomen to work with. They know how to work with others. They are fair in their judgment, and their attitude is neither indifferent nor interfering. They are appreciative of your efforts, and they do not push you aside if you make mistakes." The speaker was one who has often expressed very *swadeshi* sentiments, and it was gratifying, in these days of anti-foreign feeling, to find a quality of the best type of Englishwomen recognized and appreciated by one in no sense prejudiced in their favour.

Such working together is a mutual education and an

escape from useless criticism and bitterness. The Indian woman has great capacities for service, but she is not yet accustomed to exercising these outside the circle of her own people. She has, however, caught the vision of a larger range of influence, and in outstanding instances, like the Pandita Ramabai, Mrs. Sarajini Naidu, Mrs. Ramabai Ranade, and others, she has shown initiative and daring, and, better still, patient persistence in work not to be surpassed in the records of the West.

"When the mother heart has once awakened in them," says Sister Nivedita, "to beat for land and people, instead of family, village and homestead alone . . . then—then only shall the future of Indian womanhood dawn upon the race in its actual greatness."

In the cottage homes of Scotland one has often watched the turf fire glowing quietly without flame on the hearth. To many a Scottish Highlander the word home must bring up immediately that grateful warmth and glow. But that slow-kindling peat, cut from the moss among the hills, can burn elsewhere than in the home fires, and sometimes, lit by some mysterious spark, sets hill and forest in a blaze. It is the hardest of all fires to extinguish once it has begun to burn in the open. Some such pent-up blaze smoulders in the heart of Indian womanhood, but it will not always be satisfied to burn low on the hearthstone. A spark may set it on fire in the open, and then the world shall know all that has lain hidden in her heart.

Surely the divine spark alone is sufficient to set on fire the powers that lie stored up in the deep heart of India's women. Religion has always been the centre of their lives. There is a word used in religious poetry to describe the soul's longing for God—*biraha*—whose original meaning is the heartache of a woman for her absent husband, one of the strongest of human emotions. Without religion the Indian woman has that constant unsatisfied pain in her heart, that birana which none but the Divine One can satisfy. If she cannot carry into her new life that devotion to the "desired god" in whose service she found her peace, the benefits of her new liberty will be but Dead Sea apples.

> "If it is not my portion to meet thee in this my life, then let me ever feel that I have missed thy sight—let me not forget a moment, let me carry the pangs of this sorrow in my dreams and in my wakeful hours.
>
> "As my days pass in the crowded market of this world and my hands grow full with the daily profits, let me ever feel that I have gained nothing—let me not forget for a moment, let me carry the pangs of this sorrow in my dreams and in my wakeful hours."[1]

Thus the poet of Bengal echoes a note that runs through all the hymns of his country, and that voices the only passion that will make the life of the world worth while to the heart of India, the passion that desires through experience, whether by contemplation or by service, to reach realization of the Divine.

[1] *Gitāñjali*, Dr. Rabindranath Tagore.

INDEX